AUTHENTIC HAPPINESS

—— IN ——

Seven Emails

A philosopher's simple guide to the psychology of joy,
satisfaction, and a meaningful life

Javy W. Galindo, M.A., M.Eng.

Enlightened Hyena Press
Los Altos, CA
www.HyenaPress.com

This book is published by Enlightened Hyena Press.
2310 Homestead Rd, C1 #125
Los Altos, CA
www.HyenaPress.com

Although the author and publisher have made every effort to ensure the accuracy and completeness of information contained in this book, we assume no responsibility for errors, inaccuracies, omissions, or any inconsistency herein. Any slights on people, places, or organizations are unintentional.

This publication is sold with the understanding that the publisher and author are not engaged in rendering psychological, legal, or other professional services. If expert assistance or counseling is needed, the services of a competent professional should be sought.

First Paperback Edition
ISBN 978-0-9842239-4-7

Book Design: Raheel Ahmed
Editing: Marcia C. Abramson & Margaret Diehl

ATTENTION UNIVERSITIES, CHURCHES, ORGANIZATIONS —
DISCOUNT ON BULK PURCHASES AVAILABLE.
For information, please contact the publisher:
www.HyenaPress.com, info@hyenapress.com, (408) 329-4597

Also by Javy W. Galindo

The Power of Thinking Differently:

An imaginative guide to creativity, change,
and the discovery of new ideas

Attention Instructors

For supplementary material for courses and workshops visit
www.JavyGalindo.com/authentichappiness

Table Of
CONTENTS

Foreword

I was asked to write a foreword to this book. I'm not a writer and I really don't even know what a foreword is, except that books often have them at the beginning. I was also told that it should contain my sincere thoughts and that my thoughts are supposed to tell you something about the book that will make you want to read further.

So here goes:

It is a bit surreal thinking about how my life has changed since I first reached out to Professor Wong asking about his course on happiness. I feel like such a different person now and my days feel as if they are tinged with a little brighter color. I would like to say that the quality of my life before I began receiving his emails now seems like a distant memory. The truth is that I'm still reminded of it on a daily basis, but I feel better equipped to handle it all.

Before my initial email, I was distressed that I would never find a way to deal with what I was going through. And then our email exchanges had a rocky start.

Do you know how when you send an email to a stranger (kind of like a cold call), you have no idea how they will respond? Maybe you got their email from a friend or relative and you're asking for a favor, like, "Hey, I'm a friend of Bill and he said you had some extra tanbark you are no longer using because you've decided to lay down some sod."

Then you start wondering about their response: *will they be nice and give me the tanbark*, or *will they at least let me down easy*, or *will they ignore me*, or worse, *will they treat me like dirt?*

And have you ever had it happen that after you send the email they actually respond back to you, not just with an answer, but with another question, and they keep doing that after all of your emails? And then you never know when you should stop responding because you guys aren't really friends?

Our email exchanges, and so this book, started off like that.

To be completely honest, I thought the professor was a bit of an ass after his first few responses. And who in the world writes emails that are several pages long, anyway? Do all humanities professors do that?

But now, after having read the email exchanges again, I was the one who sounded like the ass. That's okay. It was worth it.

I also know how odd it will seem that I stopped responding to his emails for over a month. Believe me, it's not that I wasn't reading them. In many ways it was BECAUSE I was so absorbed by them, so excited to read them that I wasn't able to write back until I did. And yes, during some of the longer breaks between his emails I was worried he may have forgotten about me. Even if I could have written back earlier, what was I supposed to say to somebody who was gracious enough to share as much as he did? "Hey, Buddy, where's the rest of my free stuff?"

Other than a few minor edits, I think you'll be reading them just as I did. I am excited to know that you may be undertaking the same interesting journey that I experienced.

To help make you want to read further, I can honestly say that the seven emails in this book (more like a dozen really, if you count the introduction and epilogue) opened my eyes to the possibility of a better life. You don't need to be miserable to make use of them. I think you just need to be curious and open to new perspectives.

Does that make you want to read further? I don't know.

What I do know is that I'm so happy I had the courage to ask that one simple question that most people are not just afraid to ask because the answers seem obvious, but never really even think of asking.

What I also know is that if you are like me, after reading these emails you'll never see happiness the same way again.

With gratitude,
-Vickay D. M.

P.S. You know how sometimes you come across differently in an email than you do in real life? This idea definitely applies to me here. Please be kind and keep that in mind. ☺

Editor's note:

Though the book contains the emails as they were first written, to make it more valuable to the reader a few alterations have been made. For one, some grammar has been corrected and certain words or phrases have been emphasized with font style changes that may not have been part of the original email exchange. Two, some section headings have been added throughout to make the long emails easier to digest for the general public. And three, definitions have been added to the beginning of some chapters to better frame the discussion that follows. I hope they help.

Lastly, on a side note, I never thought Vickay sounded like an ass – at least not any more than is considered culturally normal behavior. ☺

-JW

Psychology of Happiness
(Syllabus Excerpt)

Course Description:

This course will provide an introduction to the psychology of human happiness. Students will explore the latest research in the field of positive psychology and learn practices that can be used to enhance a person's quality of living. Through lectures, discussions, videos, and hands-on exercises, students will gain knowledge of how to help themselves and others live happy, satisfying, and meaningful lives.

Course Learning Outcomes:

At the conclusion of this course, students will be able to:

- Describe the psychological roots of human unhappiness.

- Explain why happiness is more of a choice than an object to pursue.

- Teach others, or implement in their own lives, scientifically backed exercises and habits that lead to experiencing a life full of more joy, satisfaction, and meaning.

- Compare and contrast the findings of modern positive psychology with the wisdom of Eastern psychology and other spiritual traditions.

- Create a *Personalized Inspirational Guide to Well-Being* for themselves or clients.

Introduction

 Sent on 9/15/2013 10:32 AM

Dear Professor,

I heard that you teach a quarter-long course on the psychology of happiness. I have a quick question regarding this topic that I hope you can answer for me.

I'm currently a little past middle age. My life experiences have left me very confused about happiness.

I've done everything I thought one is supposed to do to be happy. I went to school, got a degree, found a high-paying, stable job, and made some good investments that afforded me a fairly wealthy lifestyle. I found a wonderful partner, started a great family, and lived in a picturesque home in a pleasant neighborhood. While we were married, my spouse developed a successful startup and we became the envy of all our friends and family.

But this did not lead to happiness.

Eventually I left my job for one with lower stress and convinced my partner that we would be happier if we lived a simpler life. But after making this drastic lifestyle change, we slowly drifted apart. I thought the opposite was supposed to happen! Eventually, I left him. (It could have been the other way around, but that doesn't really matter, right?)

So even when I stopped focusing on money and lived a more modest life, I still wasn't able to find happiness.

I was depressed for a while, but never broke down or hit the med-line. I was just caught up thinking *woe is me* until one day when I looked at the world and noticed the world isn't really happy either. People suffer every day with illness, accidents, and natural disasters. Think about all the violence in the news, all the threats of war, all the corruption, crime, greed, terrorism, etc. These are all signs of people trying to make themselves happy at the expense of others and failing miserably at it.

I see this all the time: people reacting angrily or out of frustration to trivial things, holding onto grudges, or looking at everyone as if they are about to wrong them. I constantly see people worrying about matters outside of their control, or stressing out over decisions long past, replaying them in their minds as if addicted to a bad movie, living every day afraid they'll catch a cold.

I remember a specific day not that long ago when I saw all of these happen in the span of a few minutes. A customer in line at Starbucks just blew up, screaming when another customer accidentally brushed his shoulder as he walked by. The person behind me was depressed that he was only able to afford one Grande Mocha Frappucino a week on his current salary. The couple in front of me were complaining non-stop too. The husband complained about how the line was moving too slowly for them to make it to their movie on time, while the wife was talking about how their friends at the theater were going to be so mad about their lateness. To top it off, the cashier was giving his life story to each customer, talking about how he accidentally shaved off too much of his dog's fur last night, which was somehow his mother's fault.

It just seems all so stupid. And this isn't just a one-time occurrence, professor. I see similar scenes all the time. Most people seem lame when it comes to life.

When I found out that you *taught* a class on the psychology of happiness, it piqued my interest, but I also kind of cringed. I think most people fool themselves into thinking they're happy, when they're really miserable most of the time. I just don't believe it's normal to be happy. It doesn't seem like real happiness exists for most of us. What do you have to say about that?

Warmly,
Vickay D. M.

 Sent on 9/15/2013 12:23 PM

Dear Vickay,

1 greatly appreciate your thoughtful email and the time you spent writing it.

To answer your question: I agree with you.

Thanks,
-JW

 Sent on 9/15/2013 3:10 PM

Dear Professor,

1 have to be honest. Though I don't believe in the existence of happiness anymore (or at least, long-term happiness beyond the occasional win by my favorite sports team or the momentary feeling that comes with a well-timed cigarette), I was kind of hoping you would give me a longer response that proved me wrong.

I missed the opportunity to take your course the last time you taught it, and I haven't been able to find out when you're teaching it next. So, I was hoping you'd share a few insights from your class to help me out.

But, if happiness doesn't exist, then WHAT THE HELL DO YOU TEACH!?

Warmly,
Vickay

Sent on 9/15/2013 5:23 PM

Dear Vickay,

[FYI, this email turned out longer than I had planned.
Please bear with me.]

I greatly appreciate your warmth and your curiosity on this subject.

But before you read further, if you feel like you need immediate help, rather than email me, I suggest you see a counselor. Because we are not speaking in person, it's hard for me to gauge your emotional state at the moment. Learning about my course may not be of much help if what you need is more immediate personal attention.

I am primarily a philosophy and humanities instructor who has also taught introductory psychology and statistics courses. As a humanities instructor I'm interested in questions like, "What makes life meaningful?" and "What do we value and why?" Like you, I am curious about happiness.

What I have found out with my students is that in order to engage them in course material (whether it's a discussion on Taoism, Descartes, the workings of the nervous system, or how to analyze an artifact of popular culture) I must communicate how the material will be of use to them. They need to see how the material is meaningful to what they go through in life. Oddly enough, people seem engaged when I find a way to show how the material is related to heightening their experience of happiness. I can be enthusiastic and creative with the way I teach how to find the standard deviation of data, but it still may not stir a bone in my students' bodies. But if I say, "and this is how you can make a million dollars with this knowledge" or "and this is how you can have unlimited orgasms," their eyes widen as if they were jabbed with a shot of adrenaline. I first discovered this with my introductory psychology courses. One quarter, I started to teach the course by focusing on how knowledge of all of these disparate psychology topics (psychodynamics, personality theory, perception, brain functioning, classical conditioning, etc.) can be used to help us live life *more elegantly,* as I phrased it. We often don't study how to be a more skilled life-liver as directly as we learn how to be a better mathematician and writer.

As I began to reframe the course as an exploration of how to achieve a positive engagement with life, I submerged myself in the psychological discipline where many new happiness findings were occurring – the study of positive psychology. What I found was very enlightening. I thought it would be wonderful to summarize some of the findings and help disseminate them to the public through a graduate course. So I proposed one to my department and was lucky enough to be given the chance to teach it.

However, as I said, I'm not primarily a psychologist, but a philosopher. After reviewing several studies presented in positive psychology texts, it occurred to me that this research has significance beyond the study of psychology, to philosophy and humanities courses in general.

In my graduate course, we not only explore these results objectively, we think critically about what they mean for us subjectively. We try to see how we can personalize the results, trying to make meaning of them in a way that can improve the quality of our individual lives.

My students and I also take these results and explore them in the contexts of cultural paradigms, wisdom traditions, spiritual practices, and self-help belief systems to see what place they have in a life well lived.

In a nutshell, this is what the hell I teach. ☺

Thanks,
-JW

P.S. I never said that happiness doesn't exist. I just agreed that it isn't necessarily normal in our society to be happy all the time. But why should we settle for just being normal?

Sent on 9/16/2013 10:14 AM

Dear Professor,

Thank you for your own thoughtful response.

Believe it or not, I do speak to a counselor on a weekly basis, but she isn't exactly an expert on happiness. (Part of me wonders if counselors are experts at anything, but maybe I'm just a bit hard to deal with.)

It's not that I'm suicidal or anything. I don't think of myself as a head case. I'm just fed up with the way I've been living my life. I can feel so trapped in stress, negativity, and dissatisfaction. I fall into lulls where I don't feel motivated to do much of anything other than get angry.

It often feels like I've been imprisoned by my own unhappiness.

I know you must be a busy person and, reflecting now on my past emails, I think I've been beating around the bush and have been asking the wrong questions, assuming you would know what I was really asking. I'd like to cut to the chase.

Due to circumstances beyond my control, I was unable to attend your last course sessions, and will be unable to attend any in the near future. Because of my limited access to your course, and because of all the positive things I've heard about it, I was hoping you could provide some knowledge that could help me answer one important, simple question:

How can I be happier?

Or to not seem so selfish: How can *we all* be happier? I'm not asking for the keys to Nirvana or a hand to walk me up the stairway to heaven. I'm just looking to see what you might have to say to point me in the right direction.

Sincerely,
Vickay

Sent on 9/16/2013 2:38 PM

Dear Vickay,

I greatly appreciate your honesty and your directness. I can't really impart everything we cover in the course in a single email, nor do I think anyone who claims to be able to teach people how to have a happy life through one email (or two, or three, or six emails for that matter) should be taken seriously.

You can imagine that I frequently receive random emails concerning material from the courses I teach. I usually do not have the time to provide nonstudents with responses. But fortunately, I've taken the summer off from teaching in order to work on a new textbook for my class. Your request has come at a very good time.

Let me first say that the final project for my class is for the students to design their own well-being guide: a simple summary of key ideas that resonated with them from the course that they hope to never forget. As I write my textbook, I find myself often referring to my own guide – what has resonated with me from all I've learned and taught about the psychology of happiness. To keep it simple and inspire me to take action, my personal guide is narrowed down to seven reminders: three important (and maybe counterintuitive) ideas about the pursuit of happiness and four skills for living a happy life.

This I can share with you in a series of seven emails. I'm not offering any official advice, just a chance to peek into my personal notes and see how I plan to live life a little more elegantly.

Many people just intuitively live this way. The rest of us can become so used to a life of negativity and dissatisfaction that we become resigned to it. Even if our lives aren't miserable, they aren't optimal, and we take it for granted that happiness is only an *occasional* state. You used the word "trapped," but you could also say "entranced." To escape, I think one first must open her eyes to the possibility of a better way of living. So whenever anyone shows interest in this information, I'm excited to share it.

Also, since I was the only intended reader of my guide, I left out some ideas, having already absorbed them. Now that I am using it as a basis for the textbook, I need to look again at these concepts, and decide how best to explain them to the general public. I would greatly appreciate it if, at some point after reading these lengthy emails, you could provide feedback so that I may improve my textbook. I just ask that you be patient, since I'm not sure how long it will take me to send each section.

Does this sound good to you? I can also just recommend some other books for you to read if you prefer.

-JW

 Sent on 9/16/2013 3:27 PM

Professor, I would be honored and grateful if you could share excerpts from your guide. I can't tell you how much it would mean to me, especially after finding out about your course. I'd much rather read what you have to say first before reading other books.

I will definitely provide you with feedback, but I imagine having more questions than anything else. Either way, I promise to get back to you in one way or another after reading your emails.

Thank you!
-Vickay

Sent on 9/16/2013 5:34 PM

Hello, Vickay,

I t's settled then. Over the next few emails, I will try to send some information that I hope helps you develop *your own way* of living life more elegantly.

I'll begin by first pointing out that the question you asked two emails ago, while direct, may be flawed as it makes an assumption I don't believe is necessarily true.

You asked, *What can we all do to be happier?* In a sense, I don't think people can be happier. Or at least they shouldn't focus on that.

Instead, I think people can be happy – a small, but very important distinction that I'll clarify later.

But your question is a great place to start.

-JW

Part

I

Know Thyself

Three Key Ideas to Ponder Concerning the Search for Happiness

What makes us happy?
Email

1

 Sent on 9/16/2013 7:34 PM

Dear Vickay,

How can I be happy?

Presumably when you asked me this question the other day, you realized that it's kind of a funny question to ask. Most people think they know what will make them happy, don't they?

If you look at their behavior, you can see them make choices reacting to the world in ways that they believe will make them happier – either in the short term (eat some ice cream) or in the long term (work out, go to work).

I know you mentioned that you have lived life and didn't seem to be able to find happiness. I don't believe that's true. I think you found happiness. I think that most people experience happiness all the time. The issue is that some of us experience unhappiness just as often, if not more often.

In other words, the happiness you experienced didn't stay with you as long as you would have liked. Because of this, you are continually feeling as if you are chasing happiness, trying to recapture it, or trying to maintain it. Does that sound familiar?

Let's look at what most people think about happiness. In my classes, one of the first exercises I have students do is form groups, have one member take out a piece of paper, and draw a line down the middle of the paper.

On the far right side, I ask each group to first spend five minutes writing down everything that makes them happy. The only instructions I give them are to write down everyone's ideas and to be as specific as possible, and I recommend thinking about any experiences they have had recently, even within the last 24 hours.

At this moment, I suggest doing this yourself before continuing on with this email. I'll even cue you with a little pause symbol. ☺

~

OK. Now, on the other side of the page, I ask them to write as many things as they can that make them unhappy. Again, I tell them to be as specific as possible and to think about recent experiences.

~

Let's take a look at both lists. If you're like most of my students, the lists are going to sound a lot like the song "My Favorite Things" from *The Sound of Music*.

Here are a dozen typical list items based on the dozen or so times I taught my introductory psychology course.

Happy:

- Honest spouse
- Money
- Shopping
- Beer
- A raise or promotion at work
- Sunset
- Getting a new car
- My child's smile
- Good weather
- Good tacos! Good food in general
- My favorite sports team winning
- My friends
- Nice teachers

Unhappy:

- Bills
- Bad drivers
- Rude people
- Not getting the job I wanted
- My kid crying or throwing a tantrum
- Homework/quizzes
- Cheating boyfriends/girlfriends
- My favorite team losing
- Cell phone or computer freezing
- When my boss yells at me
- Broken nails
- Dirty dishes
- Mean teachers

Are these lists similar in any way? What similarities does your list have with them? If you didn't make a list, I invite you to look at your own behaviors and ask yourself *what do I do in my life to be happier?*

Quarter after quarter, student after student, I get the same type of lists. And when I look at my own behavior, and the behavior of people around me, it's similar too.

But what is the similarity?

Here's one way to look at the list: all items mentioned are outside of us. They all refer to the conditions of our lives; our circumstances. They mention either other people – whom we really have no control over – or external things and events.

For most of us, especially in Western culture, the search for happiness is a search for hidden treasure. If I can only get _____, I will be happy. If I can only find _____, I will finally be happy. If only _____ happens, I will find happiness! To be happier, we must change the conditions of our lives.

Based on your first email, you seem to epitomize this as well when you mentioned your striving for the great education, job, financial situation, spouse, etc., and saying something along the lines of "I tried looking for happiness everywhere I was supposed to look, but couldn't find it there."

Most of us in the Western world accept this premise of happiness as fact. We may not say it to one another, though some of us do, but if you look at how we live our lives, this seems to be our guiding philosophy.

A Different Approach to Happiness

Fortunately, positive psychologists have done several studies that look to see if this approach is really the right one. After reviewing several of these studies, including studies of twins (to isolate the impact of heredity), a group of university psychology researchers arrived at a very interesting conclusion.

Psychologists Sonja Lyubomirsky, David Schkade, and Kennon M. Sheldon summarized their conclusion in the following formula for happiness:

$H = S + C + V$

H is our subjective level of happiness, S is our genetics, C is the conditions of our lives, and V is our voluntary activity (how we choose to think and respond to the world).

You can think of the formula this way. S indicates how much of our happiness level is based on heredity, C is the cards we are dealt in life or the external conditions of it, and V is how we respond to these external conditions or how we play with the hand we're dealt.

Before reading on, take a guess as to what percentage of our happiness is dependent on S? How much is dependent on C? And how much do you think our happiness is dependent on V?

~

Finished guessing?

According to the studies, here are the results:

H = S (50%) + C (10%) + V (40%)

If you're like my students, a couple of things may have surprised you here.

The first is that 50% percent of our happiness is dependent on our genes. That seems like a lot. It means that some of us are born with a tendency to be pessimistic and more prone to a gloomy disposition, while others are born with a tendency towards optimism and a more cheerful state of mind.

But that really isn't the most important result. A more important statistic is that ONLY 10% of our long-term happiness is the result of our circumstances – the amount of money we have, the type of houses we live in, the type of people that cross our paths, the cars in our driveways, the shoes we long for, or our jobs.

Now, don't misread this. This isn't to say our circumstances do not affect our long-term happiness. It's simply saying they are not as significant as genetics and our voluntary responses to life.

Take money, for instance. Research shows that raising people's income above the poverty line has a significant effect on their long-term happiness. However, the effect of money on long-term happiness after that is minimal.

Compare this idea to the fantasies many have of winning the lottery.

"Oh, how happy I would be if I were to win the lottery. I would be so much happier!"

Well, psychologists studied this too. In a famous study of 22 lottery winners, researchers compared their levels of happiness before and after winning. What do you think happened to their levels of happiness?

Immediately after winning, their levels of happiness spiked through the roof! Okay, that makes sense. But then what?

Oddly enough, after one year their levels of happiness came back to baseline. They reported being at the same level of happiness as they were before having won the lottery!

Some psychologists believe this indicates that we each have a **happiness thermostat** of sorts. There is a strong pull, based on the factors in our happiness equation (S, C, and V), towards a certain happiness baseline.

With the exception of death, most major accidents, and violent crime, this thermostat also seems to work in the other direction as well.

In one study, the levels of happiness were tracked for those who had suffered horrific accidents that left them paraplegic. It's not just that their lives were altered forever, but simple basic tasks we take for granted, such as feeding ourselves or getting out of bed in the morning, were taken away from them.

Obviously, the moment after the accident they were angry, depressed, and experienced the full spectrum of negative emotions.

Yet, the curious thing is that by the eighth week after the accident, they reported experiencing more positive emotions than negative ones, and after one year, their level of happiness was reported to be close to the baseline before their accident.

It seems as if there really is an internal pull towards a happiness baseline. But you can probably see this for yourself with your own life experiences. Think of that item you really wanted and eventually got. Or that test you didn't do very well in. Do you remember how your level of happiness may have spiked (as in the first case) and dropped (as in the second case), but eventually you came back to baseline?

Have you noticed that in general? Have you noticed those things you really wanted at the store and got gave you that high at first, but then a week or month later you were back to baseline, now craving something else to make you happy? Heck, there may even be a pair of shoes or a shirt in your closet that you were dying to have last year that's now just gathering dust.

Now, I can understand if this 10% business is hard to believe. It goes against much of what our culture believes (at least what it implicitly believes, based on movies and commercials), but think about tribal cultures who still live without modern technology. While we may stress over a bill in the mail or get upset over a slow Internet connection, they are living with the constant threat of literal, physical danger. One bad storm, one bad wound, and that's it. Those are *real* dangers to stress about. How are some of these cultures able to live happily without modern conveniences? We would certainly think that the conditions of their lives are worse than our own.

You can also think about the concentration camps during World War II. Jews in these concentration camps lived in some of the worst conditions possible, deprived of food and sleep, emotionally brutalized, under the constant threat of execution and painful, excruciating tortures. Many were not able to emotionally deal with this, and committed suicide. And who could blame them?

But what about those who persevered? How, when faced with the worst of worst circumstances, can somebody watch all of their friends and family deteriorate or be murdered yet find a way to continue finding reasons to live?

Viktor Frankl was a Jewish psychiatrist from Vienna who, with his family, was placed in these concentration camps and experienced this despair. In his book *Man's Search for Meaning* he provides this answer:

"Everything can be taken from a man but one thing: the last of the human freedoms – to choose one's attitude in any given set of circumstances, to choose one's own way."

While we can't control many aspects of our life, we can control how we respond to it. We can control how we think and how we perceive our reality.

This is where the equation is encouraging. Forget that 50% is set by genetics. Focus on the fact that 40% is determined by us. Focus on the fact that based on how we perceive our circumstances and respond to them, we can drastically change our chronic levels of happiness.

Focus on the fact that we don't have to search for long-lost treasure to be happy (or the long-lost shoes, long-lost sports car, or long-lost romantic partner, or long-lost smart phone for that matter).

Here's the first idea I'd like to pass on to you from our class:

Happiness isn't something you have to search for in life.
Happiness is a way of life you choose to have.

I'd like for you to reflect on this for a while before I send you my next email. For some, it's a difficult paradigm shift.

Instead of being able to blame the world for our state of happiness, the responsibility lies with us. For some, it's a tough idea to swallow. But, if you really think about it, it's also liberating because it means we can drastically affect the quality of our life without having to change our circumstances.

But of course, the question now is this: *If happiness is a choice, and we say we want happiness, why don't we choose it?*

Or to rephrase the question: *Why do some of us voluntarily choose to perceive the world and choose to behave in ways that keep us away from a happy life?*

There may be several possible answers to this question.

However, here's the approach I'm taking: What I'll show you in my next email is that our thoughts and actions may not be as *voluntary* as we think they are.

Sincerely,
-JW

Why do we do the things we do?

Email

2

Sent on 9/17/2013 9:47 PM

Why do we do the things we do?

This is basically the question I last left you with, Vickay.

Again, it may sound like a funny question because the answer seems obvious. When confronted with this question, most of the students in my classes simply say, "I chose to do this or that *because I wanted to choose it.*"

My question to them is whether or not that is really true. To what extent are our thoughts and behaviors the result of our conscious choice?

Scientific evidence is showing us more and more how our behaviors are often the result of unconscious thought processes. This isn't to say we are not awake when we act, but that we don't always consciously think about our behavior before doing it.

The Unconscious Mind

Sigmund Freud famously hypothesized that the majority of our psyche, our mind, lies beneath conscious awareness. It's a simple enough concept. For instance, I'm assuming at this moment that you are thinking about the words written in this email. But what if I asked you to recall your friend's phone number, what you ate yesterday, or a pleasant memory from last year's vacation? You probably weren't conscious of those things before I prompted you. But where were they before that? They must have come from somewhere.

To Freud, this implied that a lot of what is in our mind resides below conscious awareness, in the unconscious. The concept of the unconscious led Freud to one of his more famous theories: the notion that human behavior is largely the result of unmet needs and unfulfilled desires hidden in the unconscious parts of our psyche. You don't have to consciously choose to be hungry (though you could). When to feel hunger and what to do to satisfy it is programmed within us. You don't have to consciously choose to remove your hand from a hot stove. Programmed within our unconscious is the desire to do this. If we relied on conscious deliberation – *oh, I don't think this hot feeling is particularly good* – before removing our hand, our species would be walking around with some very strange-looking hands, if we were walking around at all. Survival demands the speed of instinctive responses.

Aside from this genetic programming, Freud also theorized that our personal past programs us to respond to our environment in certain ways. In particular, Freud felt that painful experiences at an early age could have long-lasting effects on our behavior. To exaggerate the point, if mom and dad accidentally left you in a shopping cart at the grocery store when you were two years old, this could possibly explain why you are irrationally fearful of abandonment by your spouse at the age of 50.

While there is some controversy over how much influence our early experiences have on our adult feelings, beliefs, and choices, there is no denying that we can be conditioned by past experience into certain habitual (unconsciously motivated) behaviors.

An adult, who as a child was bullied by a boy named Tony, may have certain defensive behaviors or painful emotions arise whenever he comes across another person with the same name. I can come to believe that my green scarf is lucky because I was wearing it the day I met my wife (assuming, of course, that I didn't wear my green scarf every day). The smell of a perfume, the style of somebody's hair, the sounds of a familiar song, a return to a familiar location can all stimulate certain responses because of our past experiences with similar stimuli.

So you see, thoughts and behaviors can occur without us choosing them. They just arise, from what some consider *unconscious* forces.

More obviously, we can train ourselves to develop habits and manifest automatic behaviors. Driving, playing a musical instrument, developing a running form, a batting stance, a golf swing – these are all examples of what we WANT to be able to do without much conscious effort. We want to make certain behaviors involuntary.

Think about all the things you need to do to get yourself out the door: get out of bed, take a shower, brush your teeth, get in the car, drive to work, etc.

How many times during the course of those events did you really make a conscious choice?

When you woke up this morning did you say to yourself, "OK, I will choose to get out of bed on this side of the mattress this morning," or did you simply get out of bed on the same side you always do without a second thought?

When you were in the shower did you consciously choose which parts to wash first or did you simply take a shower as you normally do, without a second thought?

How many times have you done any everyday task the same way you have always done it without a second thought?

Psychologists believe that in order to deal with all the stimuli around us and to handle all the choices we are confronted with on a daily basis, our brains have evolved to work efficiently. In other words, the brain is very good at doing things as if on autopilot.

Who has time to consciously deliberate about all the little decisions that make up our day? It is much more efficient for us to use behind-the-scenes processing for small, daily choices rather than engage our often unwieldy conscious awareness.

The result is that we are sometimes careless, sometimes absent-minded, and sometimes jump to wrong conclusions because we are programmed to make judgments without really thinking things through.

One way to think about this notion of behaving unconsciously is to say that our behaviors are often done out of some form of habit or instinct.

Evidence of Unconscious Choice

We already know that our brain is able to handle just about all of our basic bodily functions without our conscious awareness. We can breathe, beat our heart, circulate our blood through our veins, repair our wounds, and so much more without consciously thinking about it. In fact, sometimes our conscious awareness gets in the way of what our body does naturally. You ever have trouble sleeping because you are worried about how you are having trouble sleeping? Your body knows how to sleep, but we can get in the way of that with our conscious thoughts.

While Freud came up with his ideas around the turn of the century, modern studies also allude to the significance of unconscious processing to our behaviors.

Let me ask you this: What kind of evidence would you need to convince you that you aren't really consciously making your decisions – that you just think you are?

Take a second to think about this.

~

What if I could predict your behavior?

What if I could somehow listen to your unconscious mind and write down what you are going to do next before you consciously chose to do it? Wouldn't that imply that your sense of a conscious choice might be illusory, and that unconscious processes may be what actually dictate your behavior?

Let's take something simple. Tap your right and left index fingers on some surface, like a table. I want you to choose which finger to tap and when. I really want you to feel the choice. Maybe you'll tap LLRRR, or LLLRR, or who knows what, but the point is that I want you to feel as if you are consciously choosing to tap your fingers.

In one famous study, participants were given this finger-tapping task while inside an MRI machine so that their brain activity could be monitored.

By watching the brain, the researchers found that they could predict the participant's choices SEVERAL SECONDS BEFORE the participants consciously made their choices. Their brain seemed to know what fingers would be pressed before the participants were consciously aware of the decision.

Isn't that a bit scary?

Studies with *split brain* patients provide related results.

If you're not familiar with the term, split brain refers to a brain where the neural fibers connecting the two hemispheres (halves) have been severed – a radical surgery used to treat some cases of severe epilepsy. In some respects, it's as if the person has two brains. In a series of groundbreaking experiments, researchers found they could communicate with one half of a brain at a time, because each hemisphere only has access to one half of the visual field. Show a word on the right side of a computer screen and only the left hemisphere gets it, and vice versa.

Now, for most of us, only the left hemisphere has language/verbal capabilities. If you showed the word "music" to a patient's left hemisphere, the patient could tell you what word appeared. If you showed the word "bell" to the right hemisphere, he would say he did not see anything.

In one famous experiment by Dr. Michael Gazzaniga, the word "music" was shown to the left hemisphere and the word "bell" was shown to the right hemisphere at the same time. Then four images related to music were displayed and the patient, a man named Joe, was asked which image best related to the word he saw. Now remember, only the left hemisphere is able to articulate what it saw.

Joe pointed to an image of a church bell – the only music-related image associated with a bell. When asked why he pointed to that image rather than the other music-related images, what do you think his response was?

Here's where it gets really interesting: Joe did not say it was because he read the word "bell," nor did he say that he did not know why.

Instead, he made up a reason!

I chose the bell because I heard church bells this morning.

Think about what this means. The patient fooled himself into thinking he was conscious of the reason for his behavior, when in fact the real reason was beneath conscious awareness (the word "bell" shown only to the nonverbal right hemisphere).

It makes me wonder how many of my behaviors really are the result of *conscious* choices, and how often I'm just tricking myself into thinking they are.

Happiness and Unconscious Programming

Let's bring this all back to happiness. Take the common example of getting cut off on the freeway.

A car zooms in front of you. Immediately your pulse races, you may start to shake, spew profanity, and yell at somebody, who most likely won't hear a word you are saying.

Or take any other example where anger is triggered (a dirty look, somebody accidentally brushing against you as they walk by, the face of your least favorite politician) and ask yourself, *Did I consciously choose to react that way, or did it just happen, as if preprogrammed?*

Why would you willingly experience stress? Why would you willingly allow somebody else to trigger responses that deter you from happiness?

You may say that these are isolated cases, examples of infrequent, impulsive responses. (Though for some people, they're not infrequent at all. Surely you've met people who are angry all the time: everyone walks on eggshells around them, and every aspect of their lives suffers.) But even infrequent, such unchosen responses are bad enough, aren't they? Why not instead choose to develop the skill to avoid those reactions, or at least minimize the amount of time they hijack our thoughts?

Let's take a look at more prolonged experiences.

How many times have you washed the dishes, but instead of conscious attention being placed on the actual sensations of washing the dishes, your awareness was on thoughts about something totally unrelated?

How about when you did the laundry or when you drove to work? You ever notice that you can drive to work, take the exact same route you always do, without much conscious effort? Your mind can think of other things, wander, and sometimes you are so unaware, that at your destination you sort of snap out of a trance, a little scared that you drove fifteen miles, waited at lights, made turns, without registering any of the details? Or if you aren't as familiar with the route, you might take the wrong exit because *you weren't thinking.*

Have you noticed where your attention often drifts to while engaged in these tasks? For many, these repetitive everyday tasks are an opportunity to get caught up worrying about an imagined future or to dwell on thoughts about negative experiences from the past. Sometimes these negative experiences happened the day before. Sometimes they happened the week before. You may even find yourself getting caught up replaying negative events that occurred years earlier!!

Why do we do that? The event is over, but we continue to recall the pain, anxiety, disappointment. Why would we choose to do that to ourselves?

Evidence seems to indicate that many of our everyday unconscious "choices" – what we think about, how we perceive the world, and how to act in the world – are the result of two types of programming: genetics (nature) and our environment (nurture).

For instance, we're climbing an uphill battle with happiness from the get go because our brain was primarily designed for survival and not for happiness. Mechanisms have been passed down to us by our ancestors that give us a preference for negative emotional responses to our environment. In order to survive, we had to develop mechanisms to quickly respond to *possible* threats. So our ruminations on negative experiences, our propensity to easily anger, and our propensity to be fearful of what's to come are also programmed into us by Mother Nature. Those tendencies kept us vigilant and prepared for life-threatening problems.

We're also programmed by our environment in childhood and throughout our lives to have certain dispositions, outlooks, values, and behaviors.

The unfortunate part is that this programming is often initiated by people who are not necessarily looking out for our best interests. Fast food chains, car companies, cellular services providers, etc., are much more interested in programming us to desire their products than they are in our well-being. Television programs, films, and music lyrics can program us to desire unattainable romance or riches, or adventures we could never survive.

And even when we are influenced by people who care about us, they are not necessarily programming us to be happy. Parents, friends, and other family members may condition us to have the same fears as they do, in the name of helping us succeed or be good people. They may even help condition us to desire and value the same things that mass culture (big business) does.

It's no wonder many of us have difficulty with long-term happiness. We are constantly being pulled by simultaneous elements of culture in several different directions. Everywhere we look we find expectations (often illustrated with tantalizing images and couched in emotionally powerful language) for how to behave, what to look like, what kind of job to have, how much money we should make, etc.

When we think back to examples of people who live happily with less in rural settings, or native indigenous people who live happily off the land, we see that one reason they are happier than those in modern cultures is that they are not burdened with this sheer volume of expectations. Think about how frustrated you get when your computer or smart phone freezes or when the food at the restaurant tastes a little bit different than the last time you were there.

We weren't born with these expectations. We weren't born to desire the car and the raise, nor were we born to desire a fancy degree and nice pair of shoes.

These are programmed into us by our culture.

When we say, "I chose to do it because I *wanted* to do it," it turns out that a lot of those *wants* have been programmed into us. Even the desire for certain foods is influenced by our genetic predisposition to want salt, fat, and sugars for survival's sake.

It's also no wonder many have a misplaced view of happiness, continually thinking it exists somewhere outside us and is something we must attain or achieve. That's exactly what we were programmed to believe. Every car, beer, jewelry, Hallmark card, perfume, cologne, coffee, hamburger, and underwear commercial is telling us that happiness will be found if we buy their product. And since advertisers are subtle, they often suggest that the reason this item will make us happy is more than simple possession: there's an implication that to choose this product means we are a superior sort of person, one of taste and refinement, or one who lives dangerously, or one who is gregarious and fun-loving.

According to many popular films, television shows, and song lyrics, happiness is to be had only if we are able to find whatever it is that the protagonists find at their happy ending.

The result is that we are conditioned to believe we are flawed, that we are not fulfilled, and that there is something constantly missing in our lives. We end up having a very perverse understanding of not just how to attain happiness, but what it is.

Fortunately, we can reprogram ourselves. We aren't bound to the programming of our parents, our culture, nor even completely bound to the programming of our genes. If we are going to operate on autopilot much of the time for efficiency's sake, we might as well consciously program the route and destination.

Just as a person can train himself to develop more skillful musical habits, so too can we train ourselves to develop more skillful habits for living life. We can train ourselves to develop the habits to *choose* happiness.

Here is the second idea I'd like to pass on to you from our class:

If unhappiness is often the result of unconscious programming, maybe we can reprogram ourselves for happiness instead.

But if long-lasting happiness doesn't come from pursuing programmed desires, where does it come from?

The ironic thing is that research shows that we have it all backwards. As a result of our conditioning, we believe that if we attain the things we desire, we will be happier.

Instead, studies show that people who are happier are more likely to attract a romantic partner into their lives. Studies show that rather than money leading to happiness, people who are happier are more likely to make more money. Studies even show that rather than health having a great impact on our happiness, we are more likely to live healthier and longer lives if we are happy.

Getting what you want in life doesn't necessarily make you happy in the long run, but being happy may help you get what you want.

But if happiness isn't getting what you want, what is it then? What is happiness anyway?

Sincerely,
- JW

What is happiness anyway?

Email

3

 Sent on 9/18/2013 4:30 PM

What do you think, Vickay? Is happiness simply feeling good? Is it simply experiencing positive emotions?

Is happiness equivalent to pleasure?

At the most rudimentary level, happiness is just a word, like all others, that clumsily represents some sort of experience, a word that we can easily make associations to, but often have difficulty defining exactly.

Sure, we can give examples of when we've been happy. We can give examples of what we feel when we're happy, but that seems to oversimplify happiness and treat it as "just" an emotion, when many people will also say that it is much more than a feeling.

And since so many of us have difficulty maintaining this feeling, there may be something awry with our understanding of what it is – or at the very least what long-term happiness is.

So rather than define it first, and investigate how it comes about, why not see what it is, based upon people's responses to questions about whether they are happy? In other words, when psychologists perform studies concerning happiness, what is it that people are experiencing when they say they are happy?

As it turns out, people seem to be happy when they...

1. Experience a lack of unpleasant emotions and a surplus of pleasant emotions

2. Experience satisfaction through their activities

3. Have a sense of purpose and meaning

This may seem like common sense, but is this really how most of us approach happiness? By observing people's behavior, Sigmund Freud deduced that our primary motivations are to search for pleasure and avoid pain. This sure sounds more like how many people I know approach happiness.

The underlying belief that happiness is equivalent to feelings of pleasure is in part due to the addictive nature of experiences that bring about positive emotions. Just as alcohol and other drugs can trigger a release of positive emotional chemicals in the brain (with a corresponding hangover or painful withdrawal alleviated only by partaking again), so can shopping, achievement, recognition, and experiences of romantic love.

This isn't to say that positive emotions are bad, but rather that because they are chemically based, they will fade as the effect of the chemical fades. Hence, our feelings of pleasure are temporary at best, and can cause painful addiction at worst. (In a later email, I will even provide some ideas on how we can become more skillful at experiencing pleasure.)

This is what I find wonderful about the type of research done by positive psychologists. It's not that their insights are necessarily groundbreaking, but that they confirm and bring to public attention ideas that most of us have forgotten or have ignored.

Rather than allow ourselves to become trapped in the mindless pursuit of pleasure, often referred to as the **hedonic treadmill** in positive psychology, we can learn to behave in ways that more effectively influence our long-term levels of happiness. To begin with, we can place more attention on developing our ability to cope with negative emotions, rather than simply masking them through experiences of pleasure. We can also cultivate the skills for experiencing satisfaction with what we do with our lives. And we can develop a mindset that enables us to experience meaning and purpose.

In other words, we can reconfigure our approach to a happy life to include more than getting, accumulating, and achieving.

This leads to the third idea I'd like to pass on to you from our class:

Happiness is more than a positive emotion.
It is the state of a life well lived.

I want to point out that I don't think of this as a direct path to a *happier* life. I think of it as a way to develop the skills to living a *happy* life.

This is not to say that it is not appropriate to use the term "happier." In a sense, you can argue that if you are increasing how often you feel you are living a happy life, you are living a happier one.

However, as a person who has spent a lifetime trying to be happy (whether I was aware of this or not), I have found it more beneficial to approach happiness as a state of a person's life rather than a quality of life that has a gradient.

Like a Toyota car that can't be any more of a Toyota, I don't think we need to think of a happy life as one that could be happier.

For one thing, if we treat happiness as a quality of life that we can have more of, there is a tendency to see it simply as an emotion (a positive feeling), since to some extent emotions themselves have gradients – more pain, more sadness, more excitement, or more pleasure. We then tend to neglect the other elements (satisfaction and meaning) of a happy life.

More importantly, focusing on a happy life defined this way keeps us from the dreaded cycle of continually striving for more. If we think of happiness as something that can be increased, there may never be an end to our craving and this may lead to continual dissatisfaction and feelings of inadequacy in one way or another. We completely miss the possibilities for appreciation and enjoyment of the life we have now.

Aiming for a happier life also sounds like you are trying to make a happy life more so. But if you are already happy, then I suggest you stop looking further. It may be your longing for *more* happiness that is causing you to experience unhappiness.

Instead of thinking "happier" life, what I personally want is to have a life that is more consistently happy: to experience a happy life more often.

Do you see the small, but I think significant, difference in perspective? I think this one change in perspective can make all the difference in the world.

A Simple Approach to a Happy Life

Doesn't it feel as if we can fall in and out of a happy life pretty easily, often due to changes in our external circumstances or random streams of negative thoughts? I believe happiness is a state that we can enter into and stay indefinitely. People often don't believe this to be true because one, it seems difficult to do, and two, because they too strongly associate happiness with inherently transitory positive emotions, feelings that come and go. But if we start to see that a happy life is more than emotions, I don't see any reason why, with enough practice, we can't start to even appreciate our painful experiences as part of a happy life. In my later emails, I'll even make the case that painful experiences may be necessary to living a life full of meaning.

So what can we do when we are in those unhappy states to remind ourselves that we can choose to reenter a happy one?

In my own personal guide to well-being, I wanted a way to easily and quickly refocus myself when I found myself out of happiness.

If entering the state of a happy life really is a choice, as positive psychology research seems to indicate, then I wanted a simple way to remind myself of all the key ideas from this research.

I came up with a phrase that I can easily use to refocus myself in times of unrest. When life overwhelms me, when I get caught up in negativity, and the world seems a bit dark, I repeat to myself the following few words:

Easy, light, smooth, and meaningful.

The phrase summarizes my takeaways from positive psychology research, but it stems from a passage from a popular book entitled *Born to Run* by journalist Christopher McDougall.

The book begins with the author's search for an elusive mystery man known as Caballo Blanco who was known to live in, and run up and down, the treacherous Copper Canyon region of Mexico. In one of the more famous scenes in the book, the author finally finds Caballo Blanco, and is invited to join him on an eye-opening run through the mountains. When they begin running this challenging terrain full of steep trails, stones, and rivers, Caballo Blanco notices his new partner's difficulties and his awkward form and provides these simple words of advice:

> Think Easy, Light, Smooth, and Fast. You start with easy, because if that's all you get, that's not so bad. Then work on light. Make it effortless, like you don't give a shit how high the hill is or how far you've got to go. When you've practiced that so long that you forget you're practicing, you work on making it smooooooth. You won't have to worry about the last one – you get those three, and you'll be fast.

The power of the words is in their simplicity.

Occam's razor is a principle often used by scientists when deciding between two equally likely solutions to a problem: *choose the one that is the simplest, the one that is most elegant.* "Elegant," in science, doesn't mean what it does in the pages of a fashion magazine, although there are similarities. It means creative, economical, doing the job as simply as it can be done without losing anything important.

Long-distance trail running can be difficult, and if one were to submerge oneself into the ocean of running strategy and technical minutia, one might never emerge. So by focusing on this advice from Caballo Blanco, using it as a checklist (or mantra), a runner can easily refocus and run more effectively in that one present moment. And if those moments can be strung together, the runner finds that he's become a more effective runner. It is a solution that simplifies what some consider a complex problem.

Similarly, though I use the terms slightly differently than good old Caballo Blanco (the real-life Micah True, born Michael Randall Hickman), I think living a happy life doesn't have to be such a complex task. I think there is power in finding a simple way, or simple reminder, that I can refer back to when I lose myself in the eye of a negative whirlwind, or feel as if I am being mercilessly tossed to and fro by the constant activity of the sea of life.

Think easy, light, smooth, and meaningful. You start with easy, because if that's all you get, that's not so bad. Then work on light. Be lighthearted and live with joy, like you don't give a shit how rough the seas are or how far you've got to go. When you've practiced that so long that you forget you're practicing, you work on making all your activities feel effortless and smooth. You won't have to worry about the last one too often – you get those three, and you may notice yourself living meaningfully.

I'll describe what each of these ideas means in four separate emails. If you're serious about trying to incorporate the ideas from the class in your own life, I suggest you read each one as it comes and give yourself time to digest it. I'll suggest some exercises you can do to be more skilled at each, so you may want to try them out for few days before going on to the next reminder. In my class, we have two weeks between each session. This gives students plenty of time to experiment with these ideas.

Or you can simply wait for them all to come and read them through in one sitting. Your choice really, and you know what I think about conscious choice.

Sincerely,
-JW

Part

II

Elements for a Life Well Lived
Four Reminders for a Happy Life

Live Easy

Email

4

Easy (adjective):
Free from pain, annoyance, or anxiety.

"He had an easy disposition. He was easygoing."

 Sent on 9/18/2013 8:33 PM

Hi, Vickay,

I know I gave you a lot to process in my emails over the past few days, and not much time to respond. As I mentioned before, I recommend digesting them each over the course of a few weeks. Please feel free to ask me if you have questions, but I want you to know you need not reply back for the sake of politeness. I'll assume the emails have found their way to you.

Your prompting me for this information has really been a blessing. Before I heard from you, I was having difficulty organizing my ideas in a coherent, meaningful way. Now, knowing that I'm sharing my ideas with a specific person, the organization comes much more easily.

We're often told that life isn't supposed to be easy. Life is full of obstacles that have to be overcome, challenges that have to be faced, and hardships that we could have never expected.

I believe these people are right. The circumstances we find ourselves in can be arduous.

And often we can't do a damn thing about it. There are an infinite number of circumstances in our lives that are completely out of our control: being laid off from work, becoming ill, being hit by reckless drivers, and the list goes on.

Nobody can expect to live life void of difficulties without being gravely disappointed. But we can certainly develop skills to effectively deal with difficulties. And more importantly, we can develop the ability to not exacerbate our suffering by manufacturing trouble out of thin air, through our own imagination.

The first element of a life well lived that I've learned from my studies is to live *easy*.

Easy here doesn't refer to what life should be. It refers to an approach to life where we don't make it more difficult than it has to be.

But unfortunately for us, we are very good at doing just that.

Mindfully Managing Your Negative Thinking

Nobody can blame you for feeling pain after stubbing your toe or feeling frustrated when you suddenly find yourself with a flat tire.

However, unpleasant conditions are not the sole cause of our suffering. A significant amount of our suffering comes without being triggered *by any immediate experience at all.*

Notice how often you experience unhappiness without being provoked by the circumstances of the moment. While taking a shower, eating a meal, or during any number of neutral conditions of your day, how often did you fall out of happiness? Have you ever been engaged with something enjoyable only to have it ruined by incessant internal negative chatter that you can't seem to escape?

Our unhappiness is often self-inflicted, coming about from holding onto and replaying (and exaggerating) negative experiences from our past and pointlessly unnecessarily imagining (and exaggerating) possible negative experiences in our future.

Rather than the conditions of our lives being the primary culprit for our suffering, our own thoughts and emotional reactions are often our worst enemies.

It appears that there may be an evolutionary reason for this.

If you take a look at our nervous system, we have a built-in mechanism for quickly raising our heart rate, increasing sweat production, and other stress responses when faced with threats. In other words, our body automatically prepares us to fight (get angry) or run away (become afraid) when it senses danger. This is commonly referred to as the fight or flight response and is a function of the **sympathetic nervous system** (a subsystem of the nervous system). Our ancestors developed this stress response to marshal the internal resources to appropriately deal with possible dangers in the environment –predators, poisonous snakes, enemies.

If we didn't easily anger, or easily become fearful, our ancestors would not have been able to quickly react to signs (sounds, smells, glimpses) of danger. Obviously, those who were not able to do this had little chance of being anyone's ancestors.

Though most of us do not encounter life-or-death threats on a daily basis, we still have this reactive system. But now, instead of being triggered by a rustling in the bush or a growling sound in the distance, it is triggered by bills, mean bosses, disagreements, or a piece of paper that says "quiz" on it.

Our useful survival mechanism is being misused/overused in our more modern environments.

In order to quickly *react* to possible threats, our nervous system also developed the skill to quickly *spot* possible threats. But quickly spotting threats means being hyper-vigilant, and this has led to a tendency to see danger when none really exists. I've seen neuropsychologist Rick Hanson refer to this as the **negativity bias**.

If you heard a rustling in the bushes, it was more advantageous for survival to guess "lion" than it was to guess "wind." Better to be safe than sorry when your guesses are a matter of life or death.

But this also means we were more prone to look for possible pitfalls than to look for rewards. If our ancestors weren't starving, it was more important to notice the possible tiger behind the bushes than it was to notice the fruits hanging from them.

Most of the time, it's okay to occasionally miss seeing fruits that are right in front of your face. You can always find fruit another day. But the day that you miss seeing the tiger may be your last.

The negativity bias might then help explain the propensity to get caught up in negative thinking: it's safer to ruminate over possible problems than to focus on possible pleasures. It's a byproduct of our ancestors' hyper-vigilance. And replaying problems from the past may help us feel as if we are properly preparing for future dangers.

It's not just the thoughts themselves that cause unhappiness, but the fact that they occupy so much of our attention. In some cases it might be useful to think of issues that may arise later, but if that's all we do, we are sacrificing our enjoyment of the present moment. And unless you have a time machine, the present moment is all we really experience.

Before we know it, we get swept up in our own negativity, like being caught in the rough currents of a river.

Since these sorts of thoughts are *our own* impulsive, covert behaviors, how might we learn to be easier on ourselves?

Fortunately, the brain has the ability to interrupt our impulsive thoughts. While some primitive parts of our nervous system have an emergency hotline to our behaviors, more recently evolved parts of the brain have the capability to disrupt this path if we choose. If this weren't the case, we would react out of impulse all the time, which we obviously don't. Though it may be tough to resist the urge to take a bite out of our neighbor's hamburger (or yell at a whining child), we have the capability to override that impulse.

Studies of meditation practitioners provide us with a clue on how to develop the skills necessary to deal with the impulses of our negativity bias.

When researchers study the effects of meditative practices, they notice physiological effects, such as activation of the body's relaxation response. This is the counterbalance to our fight or flight system. However, they also see a correlation with subjective feelings of happiness.

People who meditate seem to be happier.

In order to see why this might be, let's take a simplified look at meditation. Many, though not all, practices include placing yourself in a comfortable position and then consciously attempting nonjudgmental awareness – focusing your attention without making a negative judgment about your experience. You may be asked to place your attention on your breath, on an image, or on a word that you repeat to yourself. You may be asked to focus your attention on feelings of love, kindness, or compassion. Some meditations simply ask that you become mindful of the sensations within your body or of the sounds in the room. If, or when, any judgments arise (this is boring, my shoes are dirty, last night was embarrassing), you are asked to bring your attention back to the focus of the exercise (breath, body, the feeling of love, etc.).

Through such practices, people develop important techniques for dealing with the negativity bias. They exercise mental muscles for self-awareness and for choosing the objects of attention. Like non-swimmers who impulsively freak out when thrown into a waist-level pool, we can become so caught up in our own negativity that we give up the choice to focus our attention elsewhere. If we can learn to become more self-aware, then, when caught in the currents of the negativity bias, we have an opportunity to consciously choose to get out of it.

"Hey! I see that the negativity bias is working in overdrive right now. I think I'll choose to place my attention on more neutral, pleasant, or productive thoughts."

Secondly, through all of these practices, people are conditioning themselves to experience relaxation, peace, and positive emotions. It's as if we are making positivity a habit. This may help compensate for our bias towards negativity.

Is the moral of the story that we should all learn to meditate and think positive thoughts? If it helps you to think about it that way, feel free to do so. To me, at the very least, all of this means that I should practice being more mindful of my own thoughts, and to take responsibility for what thoughts occupy my attention.

It means that I should take it easy on myself, rather than allow the negativity bias to make life more difficult than it has to be.

Of course, this is all fine and dandy when our negativity occurs as habit, without being provoked by unpleasant conditions. But when we do face actual difficulties in life, what then?

Dealing with Difficult Circumstances

Make a list of conditions in your life that cause you to suffer, or recent circumstances that have caused you to be unhappy.

If you can change it, then change it. But how much of your time is wasted being frustrated over circumstances that are out of your control?

Ever get mad at a person who disagrees with you or upset when the weather turns and ruins the BBQ party you had planned meticulously for days? What about all those times you may have cursed the traffic?

Many people get angry over things outside of their control. Anger is an emotion that can provide us with fuel to take action and make positive change in our lives or the lives of others. But if you want to feel happier and if there's no change that can be made, what use is the anger?

Why not use that emotion for something more productive, or to do something that gives you joy? Why not be on your own side, and choose a different response instead?

One reason is that we often look in the wrong direction for the cause of our negativity. If we look outside of ourselves, we can be frustrated because some circumstances are outside of our control. And if we see ourselves as the helpless victim of circumstance, we too easily give up our choice to react differently.

Our language doesn't help us here either. It is common to say things such as "that bugs me," "he irritates me," "this scares me," etc. The way we talk often assumes that something outside of ourselves imposes pain and negativity upon us. However, bad traffic and mean people don't magically inject anger and frustration into our system. These are all feelings that arise *within us*. Circumstance may trigger these reactions, but our reactions are completely our own.

This simple change in perspective allows us to step away from the role of helpless victim of circumstance and toward taking responsibility for our own happiness.

This isn't to say that we can always smile when we stub our toe or jump for joy when a person makes a disparaging remark. But, think back upon any unwanted or unpleasant event you've recently experienced. Maybe it was an unpleasant exchange with another person, an action you regret taking, or a random occurrence that altered your plans.

Now, take a moment to really reflect on where the majority of your suffering came from.

A lot of experiences in this world are painful and unpleasant. We can also make mistakes or do things we regret. But you may have noticed that the majority of our suffering doesn't come from these experiences directly, but instead comes from our own thoughts and beliefs about the experience.

We compound the unpleasant occurrence or circumstance with our own unpleasant, negative judgments about it.

Frequently, our negative judgments are exaggerated responses to our circumstances, and we have what are referred to as **cognitive distortions**. When our boss criticizes the timeliness of our work, we may feel that we are complete failures, as if this one criticism defines our entire sense of self. When we receive an unwanted grade on an exam, we can feel that our life is over, as if this one event will undermine all other aspects of our life. Or we can get depressed thinking about our current issues, believing that this set of circumstances is unchangeable and will last forever, when in fact most things, including our own feelings, are impermanent and change over time.

While painful experiences are an inevitable part of life, we often make these experiences even worse by piling on negative judgments about the experiences that prolongs their effect.

Also, if our circumstances determined our happiness, then all those diagnosed with terminal illness should be trapped in despair. But there are many who aren't. Some people, not in spite of but because of their illness, have discovered a new appreciation for life. Rather than focus on the natural feelings of grief, anger, and depression, these individuals are able to experience their lives with renewed enthusiasm, appreciating their day even more since mortality now stares them in the face. There may not be much we can do about our body's response to certain illnesses, but people have found ways to prevent their illness from ruling their spirit as well.

Recall Viktor Frankl's words, "Everything can be taken from a man but...to choose one's attitude in any given set of circumstances."

The psychological term for the skill of dealing with our difficulties is **resiliency** and many cognitive strategies have been developed to strengthen resiliency. Since many of these thoughts are cognitive distortions, judgments that are not indicative of reality, one strategy is to directly challenge them.

Does this really ruin all aspects of my life? Does this really define who I am? Is this really a permanent circumstance?

But in order to challenge them we must first be aware that we are exacerbating a situation with unnecessary judgments – awareness being the key concept once again.

You may not be able to consciously choose to end the feeling of pain when you stub your toe on a chair, but with practice you can learn to catch yourself when negative thoughts about the experience arise. You can tell yourself that rather than prolonging your misery with thoughts of hate or anger at yourself or the chair you bumped into, you'll decide to accept the pain as it is and not exacerbate it.

You may even want to make a conscious effort in the days to come to see if you can build this muscle of awareness. Try to catch yourself when you get caught up in the impulsive negativity that follows an unpleasant occurrence. That's the first and maybe most important step.

Then you can begin building the skill of willful attention. For one, you can practice challenging any negative judgments you may have.

Is my life really over because I burned the pot roast for dinner? So what if my mother-in-law wrinkles her nose? Is that going to kill me? (It can help to think about how you might behave in a similar circumstance – a dinner where a younger person made a cooking error. Would you let critical feelings show? If not, why do it to yourself? If you would – if you feel justified in criticizing others for unintentional difficulties – why is that? Do you like that about yourself?)

Maybe even more useful is to practice using nonjudgmental language when thinking about your circumstances. Instead of believing that *the idiot driver who obviously lacks all respect for me committed a heinous act by almost killing me when he cut me off on the freeway*, you can think of the scenario with more objective language.

A car entered my lane.

It may have done so rather quickly.

But perhaps an even more simple approach is to simply let go of our attachment to these judgments. You can't always stop a thought from entering your mind, but you don't have to pull out a chair and offer it a drink. Once you become aware that a negative thought is occurring, just decide to stop paying attention to it. Place your attention on something more important to you, like the tasks you hope to complete today, or how you might make your loved ones' lives a little better. If the thought is particularly intrusive, place your attention on your breathing – especially if it may have sped up as a result of your circumstances.

Your thoughts are your own. Everybody says so, so why not act as if you believe it? Place your attention on aspects of your life that you really care about, where you can actually make a positive difference.

It's no wonder, then, why the practice of forgiveness has been shown to have positive psychological effects on well-being. Forgiveness doesn't mean forgetting pain or condoning offenses. Nor does it mean that you downplay the seriousness of an offense. At the very least, forgiveness is the choice we make to not let the pain define us. It means letting go of the need to cling to the pain and allowing yourself to focus your attention elsewhere so that you can move on with life.

Living *easy* can refer to forgiving ourselves and our conditions, including forgiving the chair that *intentionally* stubbed your toe.

Ease Up Your Load

If much of our unhappiness is a result of our negative thoughts, and if many of these are the result of programmed mechanisms for surviving on the African savannah a million years ago, how do we account for studies that show that some present-day indigenous cultures experience less stress than many modern societies?

They live closer to nature and face life-threatening conditions more frequently than industrialized cultures. Common sense would lead us to believe they should be more stressed out, not less.

One of the issues we face as part of an "advanced" culture is an abundance of expectations. Our parents, our peers, our commercials, our movies, our television shows, and our music all program us to have an abundance of expectations about what a "good" life is about and how life should work.

Though we may not deal with life-threatening dangers very often, we interact with so many more people and our lives are so much more complex (with many more expectations), that our nervous systems may feel they need to be more vigilant than ever before.

How many of us get disappointed and frustrated when our car stops, our smart phone freezes, the air conditioner malfunctions, or when we have to wait a little long in the waiting room of a doctor's office? Compare that to those indigenous cultures that live without cars, without mobile communication devices, who rely on a breeze for cool air, and who have no access to modern medicine.

Aside from the sheer number of expectations we have for ourselves, popular culture tends to program us with expectations that are outside of the realm of possibility. These touch on all aspects of our lives including our appearance, our financial status, our relationships, and more. We then can find ourselves with a poor self-image and feelings of inadequacy, because we aren't perfectly beautiful, outrageously rich and famous, unbelievably talented, or adored by everyone. But even more importantly, as I mentioned in an earlier email, these cultural influences do not necessarily provide us with expectations *for our own benefit*. These expectations are not meant to bring us happiness.

In those moments when you feel overwhelmed, ask yourself if the expectation you are currently trying to meet is aligned with what you value in life. Is the goal you are pursuing really where you want to be? If you can pare down your expectations so that you are only pursuing endeavors that truly make you happy, your life may naturally feel more meaningful, regardless of whether you meet your goals or not.

So, to be easy, you may want to lessen your expectations of yourself and of the world around you. You may also want to decrease the number of goals you are pursuing at the present moment. It is great to have long-term goals, but we can't expect ourselves to achieve all of them at once. And, lastly, you may want to evaluate how you are living your life and focus on meeting the expectations that you truly value.

Of course, one issue is that many of us are not aware of what we authentically value. Culture has been such an influential force in our lives that we've lost sight of what truly makes us happy.

I will discuss in more detail later how you may want to figure this out for yourself. Meanwhile, positive psychologists have performed studies that we may be able to use as a general guide. Instead of striving for financial wealth and material goods, studies show that strong social networks are a much more significant factor in our happiness.

Curiously enough, when you look at rural communities and the happiest industrialized countries in the world, these are the sorts of expectations they prioritize above all others.

Learning to Live Easy

Living easy is probably the most difficult happiness habit to develop since you are retraining a brain programmed by evolution and by decades' worth of life experiences.

To build this skill you may need to remove yourself temporarily from people and activities that work as negativity triggers (talking to a certain relative, reading news articles about the economy). You're not giving these up forever or completely. If your relative calls, you'll return her call when you're ready. These do not have to be prolonged absences. Just do what you can. You can even start by simply giving yourself a few minutes of solitude in the mornings or evenings before bed.

Just remember, like a novice surfer, don't expect perfection and a smooth ride right away. Be satisfied with small, steady progress, beginning with simple awareness of when you become lost in moments of negativity. All you need is a small crack through the dark cloud, and you can begin to slowly build that muscle of awareness.

And don't forget to be easy on yourself throughout your development.

-JW

P.S. This email turned out much longer than I anticipated, but as I said before I have most of this material already composed in my personal wellness guide and within the draft of the textbook I'm in the process of writing. I hope you take the length as a sign of my enthusiasm for this material.

You have also caught me at a good time, as I'm currently on break between academic quarters. However, I fear that I may not have enough time to provide you with all the responses before the start of the fall session which begins on Monday, next week.

Rest assured, regardless of whatever delays may occur before my next email, that I am still enthusiastic about sharing this information with you.

Live Light

Email

5

Light (verb):
Animate, brighten.

" A smile lit up her face."

 Sent on 9/20/2013 7:37 PM

Hi, Vickay,

My last email may have been my most important one. Living easy may be the only reminder you need. For those who do not have happiness as a habit yet, awareness and skillful attention really are foundations for developing the skills necessary for a happy life.

These are skills that I struggle with on a daily basis and will probably continue to all my life. Fortunately, constant effort leads to progress, though it may be gradual. And experiencing gradual progress may be as good a sign of a happy life as any other, an idea I we will reflect on when discussing a meaningful life in a later email.

But when you reflect upon the quality of life you want, is it only a life free from stress, fear, and anxiety?

Should a life well lived simply be about breaking through the dark clouds of our own making, or should it also include experiencing joys; the natural bright moments of life?

When people are going through difficult times, I often hear them say that light exists at the end of the tunnel. But why wait when psychology tells us that every moment has the potential for joy if we choose to experience it?

Living *light* is a concept I use to remind myself that in every moment I can make a choice to brighten up my own day and the day of those with whom I interact. It helps me to become more aware of how I am experiencing life. This then gives me the choice to pay attention to the world in a way that allows me to enjoy it.

If you practice living easy, joyful experiences may spontaneously occur: moments where you snap out of your normal state of mind to say, "Damn, that tastes good!"

But this can be difficult to do for many reasons.

The Problem with Pleasure

Pleasure has gotten a bad rap. While experiences of pleasure may not be all there is to happiness, a life devoid of the pleasures of the senses is a rejection of a significant percentage of human experience. Why not enjoy your cup of coffee, a good meal, or the sound of your favorite band?

One issue is that even the wisest of us can become addicted to pleasure. We can become so trapped in the unconscious pursuit of pleasure that we chase after experiences without any conscious regard to whether they will really make us happy, or even give us much pleasure at all. If something really felt good at least once, we may become conditioned to believe it to be a continual source of potent pleasure, even if our more recent experiences of it tell us differently.

As Harvard psychologist Daniel Gilbert discovered through his research, we are horrible at predicting our future emotional states.

Science has even shown that experiences like shopping and romantic love can trigger the same release of pleasure chemicals in our brains as does cocaine. It's no wonder some of us become addicted to these pursuits, spending far more than we can afford, or chasing new love at the expense of a stable relationship. We deceive ourselves into expecting these quick highs to lead to a happy life. Or even if we don't believe that, we are fooled into expecting the pleasure to keep coming in the same way and with the same efficacy. In either case, we end up behaving in ways that may be detrimental to experiencing happiness.

Our addiction to pleasures may be at least partially the result of misplaced drives: behaviors that attempt to mask or compensate for the real needs that we fail to address.

Here is a basic model of the cycle of motivation that is taught in my introductory psychology classes.

Needs →Drive →Response →Goal →Reduced Need

What moves us are these feelings that we call **drives**. These emotions are the fuel for movement (e-motion).

For example, if you need water, you'll begin to feel the drive called thirst. Freud would say that feeling thirsty creates an uneasy tension that may compel you to respond, hopefully by drinking water. And by drinking enough water you reduce the original need. If your body needed water, but didn't generate the feeling of thirst, you might never address this need.

According to psychologist Abraham Maslow, in addition to biological needs, we also have emotional needs for safety and security, love and belonging, among many others. If a person feels depressed or unfulfilled, it could be the result of any number of unmet emotional needs. But when we feel a drive, we don't always realize what need may be causing it. Even the drive of thirst is sometimes confused with hunger. And instead of spending time reflecting on the underlying reasons for these feelings, we sometimes take a shortcut, masking them with quick experiences of pleasure.

Think about how some people turn to food or sex as ways of dealing with emotional needs. By neglecting to address the underlying problem, people set themselves up to experience a repeated feeling of "need," which gets translated into cravings for food and sex. The drives are masked and put on hold, only to appear again later. And the cycle continues with the person never finding satisfaction.

That's why *living easy* comes first, so that we don't become addicted to feelings of pleasure in order to deal with our negativity.

Our addictions are not just limited to sensory experiences. We can become addicted to the pleasures of status and pride that come with the attainment of wealth, achievement, or material possessions.

Addiction to pleasure can be detrimental because it lures us down false paths to happiness. But this addiction can also make your experience of pleasure less potent. An addiction to pleasure can lessen your ability to experience pleasure!

Do you remember the first time you tasted a new, amazing dish? Or the first time you tasted a magnificent glass of wine? Or the first time you heard a particular song?

What happens if you ate the dish for every meal? Or tasted the wine every hour? Aside from intoxication, you'd notice that your appreciation for it faded. The fiftieth bite of ice cream is never as delicious as the first.

This is referred to as **sensory adaptation**. The more we are exposed to the same stimulus, the less reactive we are to that stimulus. We then become habituated to it.

As a result, as we've seen in our culture, this can lead to the continual pursuit of *more*. Since our experience of something fades over time, we will desire a greater experience of it to compensate; more bites of the ice cream or new flavors, more cans of beer or – why not – tequila shots, more accolades, more money.

As we attain the goals we pursue, the less and less potent the experience becomes. And unless we realize this, and make the conscious effort to stop our pursuit, we may find ourselves continually chasing after more.

As you may have noticed from your own experiences, this unending chase doesn't necessary lead to more happiness. Always wanting more is a surefire path to dissatisfaction and frustration because pursuing "more" is an endless task. There's always "more" to be had. It's also always more difficult than simply appreciating what you have.

This never-ending chase is what is referred to as the **hedonic treadmill**.

When caught on the hedonic treadmill we are once again making life more difficult than it has to be.

Delayed Gratification

Hence, what we can develop is a more conscious relationship to pleasure. We can become more skilled at experiencing it. On one hand, this may mean that you learn to make use of **delayed gratification**. Rather than fall prey to impulsive cravings for certain experiences you really enjoy, practice spreading out your experience of them. You might love your daily cup of coffee or jelly doughnut, but you may love them even more if you practice delaying your experience of them.

On the other hand, don't be afraid to experience pleasure. If you know you love petting your dog, walking in the woods, reading a certain author, watching a television program, or listening to a certain band, find ways to incorporate these experiences even more into your daily life. You may even want to use them for incentives, turn them into rewards for a hard day's work or for reaching personal goals. Taking time to honor yourself and appreciate any progress you make towards goals is very important for feeling fulfilled because this attention makes you aware that your actions matter.

Try it for yourself. See if pushing your 11 a.m. muffin to the afternoon, and eating it more slowly, makes you appreciate it more. See if having wine twice a week rather than every night makes you taste the vintage in a way that you'd forgotten about.

This strategy has the added benefit of making your life full of experiences to look forward to. Many people fall into ruts because they don't see anything positive on the horizon. By using delayed gratification you can give mundane moments of your life renewed vigor by planning out simple joys in advance. Some might interpret this as intentionally denying yourself the pleasurable experience now, but I think of it as giving yourself the gift of greater joy later.

Joy from Within

When people give themselves a reprieve from the hedonic treadmill, even for just a brief moment, they often find that their approach to happiness was all wrong. Remember, this chase often leads us into pursuing positive feelings outside of ourselves, but just like with negative emotions, positivity is something that arises within us – not injected into us by an outside entity.

Research indicates that our experience of joy can be enhanced by expressing gratitude, savoring positive occurrences, learning to be more optimistic, developing a sense of wonder, and by taking on a more lighthearted perspective. As you can see, a more skillful experience of joy is not so much about *what we bring into* our lives, but *how we experience* what already exists in our lives.

Gratitude

In your initial email to me, you mentioned very little of the positive experiences in your life, though I know they must have been there. There must have been moments amongst the stumbles where you stood tall and experienced happiness.

I also bet that you simply were too preoccupied with other things to notice positive experiences you could have had. We do not often appreciate our experiences because our mind has a tendency towards dwelling on dangers and problems rather than rewards and solutions. And because we have a bias toward feeling fear and worry rather than peace and joy, over time negativity can become our default experience of life.

We can counter our negativity biases by developing memories of positive experiences. We can develop the habit of seeing positive attributes that are inherent in the world, but that our survival-optimized nervous system blinds us to.

This may seem like an impossible task, especially for those who see their lives as comprised only of negative circumstances. But stop for a moment and take inventory. There were an infinite number of things that had to work well, circumstances that had to go right, to place you in this position rather than a worse one. Imagine that 10 years ago you had an accident that left you unable to walk, and today you were suddenly healed. Wouldn't the mobility you now take for granted feel like a miracle? Chances are, nobody called this morning to say that someone you love has unexpectedly died. That's a great blessing. Unfortunately, we are programmed too well to focus on what hasn't gone right.

To balance this programming, one simple approach is to intentionally focus on memories of positive circumstances. This means to intentionally dedicate moments in your days to be grateful. Studies performed by Robert Emmons out of UC Berkeley indicate that a simple daily exercise of expressing gratitude can have long-term effects on our happiness. The benefits are plentiful for those who are consistently grateful. They include being more energetic, more helpful, less anxious, less lonely, and less depressed.

It might be hard to find reasons to be grateful, especially if you're so used to focusing on all the things that have gone wrong in your life. Nobody can force positivity, but the sources for it are in abundance. We can easily be grateful for grand events that take place as a result of our efforts or out of the blue. But we can also appreciate all the little things that we experience on a daily basis.

Some of us are just not accustomed to reflect on our experiences this way. Due to sensory adaptation, and a mind more focused on dangers, we often become habituated to the simple pleasures of life.

We can learn to appreciate the warmth of the sun, a meal we ate, or the bed we have to sleep on. We can be thankful for those who invented all the conveniences of our life, as well as what we consider necessities. We can be grateful for those who support us, the random smiles or kindness of strangers, or simply appreciate all that had to go right in order for us to be alive. If you simply think about the delicate complexities of your own body – your complex brain, your beating heart, your breathing lungs – how can we not be grateful? Even if you have issues with these systems, the fact that you can read this email at all means they are working relatively well.

If you think about all those whose conditions of living are worse, you may quickly see how much you have to be grateful for.

You can make this a practice by scheduling time once a week to express gratitude through a letter to yourself, by sharing your feelings with others, or through silent reflection. You can make lists of large events or small things that you may have taken for granted in the past. You may even be compelled to keep a journal and make a nightly practice of writing down three things that have gone right for you in the last 24 hours.

Just do what feels comfortable, and vary your practice to avoid it becoming stale.

What you will hopefully soon realize is that more things have gone right in your life than not.

Savoring

In addition to sensory adaptation, one of the reasons gratitude can be difficult is that unpleasant memories are often stronger than pleasant ones.

It's easy to see why. Think about your relationship between pleasant and unpleasant experiences. Which one do you linger on more?

When negative experiences occur we tend to dwell on them.

When positive experiences occur we often quickly move on, as if in a rush to the next experience. In general, our body thinks that danger needs to be remembered more strongly than reward because forgetting something that went well won't kill you, while forgetting about something dangerous can. So when we reflect on our day, week, or month, it's usually the negative memories that come to the surface.

It's no wonder then that psychological studies indicate that the simple act of savoring positive experiences can have a dramatic effect on our happiness. How often are you in such a rush to finish your meal that you fail to notice how the food tasted, much less how enjoyable it was? How often are you in such a rush that you fail to enjoy the luxury of your warm shower?

Enjoy the warmth of your blanket at night, or the smell of a cup of coffee. Don't just let them pass you by. Try to luxuriate in your senses.

Soak in the joys of a beautiful day, deeds you've done for others, and the generosity of others to you. Savor the laugh of a child, or the pink yawn of your cat, or the excellence of skill displayed all around you. Relish your workouts completed, tasks done, goals accomplished, regardless how small. Learn to savor the little steps that have to be taken to get to where you want to go.

Studies show that positive emotions need not be intense or long-lasting to be effective. When you have any positive experiences, you can exponentially increase their potency by savoring them.

Every moment of your day is full of experiences that can be appreciated and savored. All that is required is your choosing to do so.

Optimism

In addition to being programmed to focus on what hasn't gone right, we are well programmed to focus on what CAN go wrong.

To compensate we can learn to spend more time imagining positive outcomes and future events. We can make a conscious effort to be more optimistic.

Making optimism a habit can be difficult. Our brains have become so fixated on avoiding threats and preparing for possible danger that we almost forget the fact that we really never know what the future holds. The future is completely open. Almost anything can happen.

For the pessimistically inclined, instead of looking forward to the fruits of unique and challenging endeavors, we succumb to the voices that say *oh it's not worth it* and *nothing good will come from trying*. We then limit our experience of a joyful life. If we can simply realize that we are not fortune-tellers, we can experience the thrill of an open life, where wonderful accidents, unexpected gifts, and unexpected joys are always possible.

Happy surprises happen all the time. We just don't often put any effort in remembering them. And sometimes they occur, but we don't see them.

Basic psychology of perception tells us that we see only what we are prepared to see. Have you ever bought a new bike and suddenly noticed that there were tons of bikes on the roads, or bought a new car and then suddenly noticed so many of that make on the roads?

If we want to experience all the joys and positive occurrences that life has to offer, we have to be prepared to see them. We need to stop focusing on the possibility of the tiger behind the bush so we can finally see the fruit that hangs from it.

You may even want to allow yourself the freedom to dream big. It's not the fulfillment of the dream that is important. It is the cultivating of a positive outlook that will brighten your vision and allow you to see the opportunities and rewards that were always available to you.

It's important to note that optimism is not about being unrealistic. Being pessimistic on a continual basis is unrealistic. Being optimistic refers to being open to *all* the possibilities that await us in the future and not just the ones that cause us pain.

Continuous pessimism can lead people to have very defeating **explanatory styles**. For example, some people will always blame negative experiences on themselves: *it was my fault* or *I must have done something wrong.* And when positive experiences occur, they see them as the result of happenstance or external forces, rather than their own actions. These are all limiting narratives that make us feel as if we have no control over our own happiness

Optimism is about choosing narratives that give you more control. Optimism enables you to see events in more empowering ways by simply being neutral and open to more possibilities.

This may help explain why optimists often are better able to maintain high levels of well-being during times of stress, as psychological studies indicate.

For this reason, your positive outlooks and grand dreams will shine a light onto your reality, allowing you to see more of it, not less. And if nothing else, placing attention on something other than the clouds of negative possibilities provides a brief reprieve from a darkened existence.

Awe

Learning to be optimistic isn't the only way to experience this reprieve. I'm sure you've experienced the feeling spontaneously, without any effort of will.

Do you remember those times when you were so enamored by an experience that you in stood breathless wonder? It may have been the vastness of a night sky full of stars, the beauty of a tranquil forest, the depths of a grand canyon, the immensity of an ocean, or the magnificence of a golden sand beach.

In these moments it's hard to focus on negative possibilities because we are faced with the truth that the world is too grand, vast, deep, immense, and magnificent for us to claim to ever know what will happen in the future.

This is what I think about the experience of awe, and to me, it is the most real of experiences. In awe we don't see the world through the tainted eyes of a species trying to survive, but through the eyes of a child seeing life for the first time.

Unfortunately, we rarely allow ourselves the opportunity – unless hit over the head – to experience awe, though every moment of the day we are surrounded by a world that is awe-inspiring. What are your memories of awe? Most likely they are attached to childhood, youth, falling in love, or vacations in beautiful places. But they don't need to be limited to that. Every science class is potentially a class about awe, as students learn to appreciate the intricacies and complexities of the natural world. The same is true of any humanities and literature course, as students learn to see the world through the eyes of a poet, philosopher, mystic, or musician.

Those who have recovered from life-threatening illness or who have survived tragic accidents can often attest to the awe-inspiring experience of simply waking up in the morning pain free or being able to go to the restroom unaccompanied. There are numerous activities that we take for granted that others would give the world to experience again.

So to live *light* is also learning to shed light on the grandness of a life and of a universe that our mind shrinks for ease of use.

Lightheartedness

One way to make ourselves more susceptible to the experience of awe is by becoming more accustomed to seeing the world through many different lenses.

Curiously enough, the best way to do this may be by experiencing the joys of lighthearted living.

It is pretty well known that laughter increases release of feel-good brain chemicals (endorphins and dopamine), while limiting the release of stress chemicals like cortisol. But understanding a joke also exercises the part of the brain that is responsible for holding multiple meanings and perspectives. These are also the faculties needed to transcend the literal, dominant perceptions of the negativity bias that keep us away from other more positive ways of experiencing the world.

Support for this may be seen in studies of widows from UC Berkeley and Holocaust survivors from the University of Tel Aviv. A UCB study found that widows who were able to laugh within weeks of their loved one's passing were more prone to positive emotions two to four years later. Research out of the University of Tel Aviv found that Holocaust survivors often referred to the use of humor as a key to surviving their traumatic experience.

Some see these findings as evidence that laughter is a luxury, a nice distraction from the realities of life. I think this couldn't be further from the truth. Instead, these studies indicate to me that humor is critical for experiencing the full reality of life.

We can make laughter more than a luxury by savoring humorous moments when they occur, being grateful for the laughs we've experienced in the past, and by learning to develop a lighthearted perspective. This perspective entails taking a bird's-eye view of your circumstances. This means learning to laugh at your mistakes. And it means remembering that a humorous perspective may just be what you need in any moment, not just to feel better but to see reality more clearly.

This does not imply devaluing life or treating its elements as any less important. It means valuing the quality of your life so much that you learn not to take yourself or life too seriously.

Living Light

The ancient Greek philosopher Epicurus described a good life as one with pleasures AND freedom from suffering. Some take this to mean he was hedonistic, when he was really an advocate for appreciating life's simple pleasures – a good meal, a good conversation with friends. And even the word "hedonism" comes from an ancient Greek word that means "delights" or "to be delighted."

Why not spend as much time experiencing pleasures and joys as you do trying to live free of pain and sorrow? The world is full of delights that we fail to appreciate because we place our attention elsewhere, caught up in addictions that distract us from experiencing them. And we fail to appreciate the inherent joys of life because we choose alternative ways to experience reality.

When you allow yourself to experience pleasure in a healthy way, when you allow yourself the perception to experience joy, you are not just providing yourself with a moment of positivity. You provide yourself with positive memories that you can draw upon later, when you are faced with the inherent difficulties of living life. Living light doesn't just make life more pleasant, it helps develop resiliency for when circumstances are so arduous that all you want is for life to be bearable.

Moreover, developing this sort of approach to life allows you to be a light onto others. Lighten up your life, and you will naturally help lighten up the lives of those around you.

As an extra bonus, studies show that joy is magnified when shared.

You can share your gratitude of life *with* others and express your gratitude *for* others. When you savor your experience, share your thoughts and feelings with others – or better yet, share the experience itself.

This may not feel effortless at first. Living easy and light requires practice in exercising mental muscles. These are the muscles needed to become more conscious during the times we get caught up in habitual thoughts and the capacities for directing our attention elsewhere. But since we are learning how to direct our attention away from negative judgments about our circumstances and towards joyful appreciation, it's counterproductive to be critical of our difficulties with developing these muscles. Instead, think of any difficulties as the weights of your exercise. Try to let go of any expectations about your practice. Being patient with yourself and allowing yourself to be okay with your struggle will make the process actually flow more smoothly.

And as I will write about in my next email, living *smooth* is itself an element of a happy life, one beyond pleasure and pain. It's the characteristic of engaging in your activities in a way where life becomes more satisfying – something I hope you're experiencing to some extent through these emails.

-JW

Live Smooth

Email

6

Smooth (adjective):
Even and uninterrupted in flow or flight.

Sent on 10/7/2013 6:10 PM

Hi, Vickay,

I apologize for this delayed email. With the start of the fall quarter, I have found myself swept up in preparing for classes and getting back into the groove of teaching after my summer off.

Can you recall times when life seems to have just carried you along? Sometimes it feels rough, like life is pushing and pulling you as you clench your teeth, struggling to deal with everything thrown your way.

But sometimes, as it was for me during the first week, it carries you in such a way that you lose yourself in life, negative thoughts dissipate because you have no room for them in your awareness, and you seem to be in a natural movement with life. You lose track of time; day turns into night in a blink of an eye. You're so engaged with what you are doing that you forget to eat. Everything you do naturally pours out of you, as if on automatic. And it all feels so right.

This is what I would like you to keep in mind when you think about the idea of *smooth*.

It is when your attention is so engaged in life that your consciousness is not interrupted by information (including thoughts of doubt and fear) that doesn't help you towards your goal. It is when your consciousness works smoothly. Some call it a peak experience. Athletes call it being in the zone. Some more spiritual individuals frame it as an ecstatic experience.

For many of us, it happens seemingly by accident. But if we learn about what it entails, and choose to pay attention to it, I believe we can make our entire lives feel more like this.

Our lives can feel smooth.

What I have discussed in my last two emails is about becoming more skilled at managing our **covert behaviors**. *Covert* refers to internal activity that can't be seen, such as our emotional reactions, thoughts, and perceptions.

But what about our **overt behaviors**? To have a greater probability of living a happy life, how do we engage the world in a way where we feel great satisfaction with what we are doing, an experience beyond pleasure and the absence of pain?

The answer may be a single-minded state of focused motivation known as *flow*.

Flow

In the '80s and '90s Hungarian-born psychologist Mihaly Csikszent-mihalyi gave several thousand participants pagers (or like devices) in various studies to see at what points in their day they were happiest. Csikszentmihalyi would randomly page the participants asking them what they were doing and how they felt at the time. Through this, he was able to collect tons of descriptions of how people felt when they were happiest and what activities they were participating in when they felt this way.

What do you think he found?

Where and when were people the happiest? What do you think they were doing at the time? Take a second to reflect on this question for yourself. *When you want to be happy, what do you dream of doing?*

~

Do you think the participants were happiest when they were relaxing at a beach, experiencing the pleasure of a glass of wine, or watching a movie?

As it turns out, people were happiest in almost opposite circumstances. Instead of being happiest while relaxing and being passive, people reported being happiest – having **peak experiences** – while they were fully engaged with an activity.

He found that people were happiest when they were participating in an activity that was challenging, yet not so easy that it produced boredom. These activities had end goals and the participants got regular feedback that they were progressing towards those goals.

Interestingly, the descriptions people gave of what these peak experiences felt like were all similar, though the activities they were participating in at the time of the experience may have been vastly different. The peak experience that one person felt from riding a motorcycle was similar to descriptions from people who were swimming, meditating, or playing chess. They all commonly used phrases such as *I lost myself in it* and *my sense of time disappeared* and *it felt as if I was on automatic.*

What seemed to have struck Csikszentmihalyi the most was his subjects' frequent use of the word "flow" to describe their experience, as in *it just naturally flowed through me* and *it felt as if I was simply in the flow.*

These descriptions echoed the descriptions of peak experiences given by creative artists, professional athletes, and other professional groups Csikszentmihalyi studied in the '60s and '70s. Oddly enough, feelings of pleasure weren't often included as part of the peak experience. Instead, words like *satisfaction* and *gratification* were more often used.

Through his studies, Csikszentmihalyi noticed that flow can occur while someone is running, writing a poem, molding a sculpture, or singing a song. It can happen when someone is in conversation with a friend, participating in a sport, or preparing a meal.

And to the surprise of many of my students, these peak experiences often occurred while people were working!

Ordered Attention

Csikszentmihalyi's explanation of this is very interesting and it revolves around the idea of **ordered attention.**

Try this experiment: Look around the room you're currently in. What does it look like? Listen to any sounds around you. What do you hear?

Now try to focus your awareness on physical sensations of your hands or legs. What do you feel?

Did you notice that as you shifted the focus of your attention, you couldn't place full attention on all of your sensations at the same time? We can only pay attention to a limited number of things at once. We may be able to quickly shift our attention and feel as if we're conscious of more than one thing at a time, but for the most part our consciousness is a single spotlight of awareness.

Now reflect on any actions you have taken lately: maybe brushing your teeth, taking a shower, washing your clothes. Whether we are aware of it or not, we are often moved to act by some sort of goal. It could be a specific goal such as wanting to be clean for work or generic goals like wanting to be happy. But think, what would happen if you were to accidentally step in dog droppings or if a passing bicyclist splashed muddy water all over you? This information may conflict with your goals, so some amount of your attention may be disrupted, diverted towards eliminating the *problem*. The more disrupted we allow our consciousness to become, the greater our **psychic disorder**.

You can think of psychic disorder as a scattering of our attention. Imagine trying to do a mindful walk through a windy field. If your attention keeps being disrupted by your attempts to keep every strand of your hair in its proper place, your walk will be more aggravation than contemplation. Csikszentmihalyi believes that pain, fear, rage, anxiety, jealousy all are the effects of psychic disorder.

Flow, then, is the state where attention can be freely placed on achieving one's goals because there is no psychic disorder to disrupt it.

Notice though that flow isn't about the absence of difficulty or hardship. Instead it refers to the quality of consciousness one brings to an experience. It is a state where we are so focused that our mind expertly rides the river of life rather than fights against its currents.

Work, as with most other activities, can give us the opportunity to experience this flow. We can get so caught up in a task or activity that we lose ourselves in it.

But as you've probably experienced, psychic disorder can occur when we face a task that's too difficult, or engage in an activity that's too easy. We can experience psychic disorder when our own critical judgments disrupt our focus. Thinking *this job sucks, I deserve to make more money, I should have received the promotion,* or *this is a waste of my skills,* are some of the most common perpetrators of psychic disorder.

Our own thoughts about our activity are often more responsible for preventing flow than the activity itself.

Learning to Enter Flow

Csikszentmihalyi's studies show us that we can choose to approach our activities in ways that naturally put us into states of ordered attention. We can skillfully engage with the world so that we are less prone to the critical judgments that disrupt our focus.

In other words, we can learn to consciously enter states of flow.

Having Clear Goals

One of the most common characteristics of flow experiences is clarity of intent. People in flow have meaningful goals and a clear sense of purpose in mind.

When basketball players are in flow, they are clearly focused on outscoring their opponents. When chefs are in flow, they are clearly aiming for particular tastes, smells, and textures. When a surgeon is in flow, he is clear about all the steps of the procedure and what it needs to accomplish.

When you are participating in a task you have a greater chance of entering flow if you are clearly aware of what it is you are trying to achieve and why. If this isn't apparent in your activity, you can give yourself an achievable goal, regardless of whether it is inherent in the activity or not. And you can find ways to constantly remind yourself of the overarching purpose of your activity. I used to teach at a college with older students who were returning to school after several years (and sometimes decades) away from a classroom. They would sometimes get discouraged by how hard it was to return, but would also find renewed vigor when they reflected on why they were doing it: to give their child a better life, to provide better support for their aging parents, or to simply improve their current quality of living.

Following Intrinsic Motivations

Research also indicates that it is easier to enter flow states when people are doing things that they are naturally interested in. Those that experienced flow while performing music performed for the love of making music. The same is true of flow in activities such as playing sports, dancing, or working on a car. Can you recall having this type of experience doing an activity you naturally love?

If you are doing something that doesn't naturally excite you, you can make it exciting if you find a way to make use of your most cherished skills. For example, I love using my creativity. Since I'm a teacher, I often find myself in flow when I try to develop my lesson plans, experiment with unique and creative ways of explaining difficult concepts, or when I put together visually interesting slides. Whatever skills you enjoy using, find ways to approach your activity so that you use them.

You can also motivate yourself by approaching your activity in a way that includes or takes note of virtue – of what you value and want to see more of in the world. If you value kindness, and you work with people, there are myriad ways to make kindness an essential part of your job. If you value courage, engage yourself in the job in a way that tests it. *I'm going to go into that meeting and (respectfully) say exactly what I think the project needs.* If you value wisdom, remember that every moment of life is a learning experience and this activity or job has things to teach you right now that will never be repeated.

By taking these approaches to life, participating in any activity becomes an end in itself. As Csikszentmihalyi terms it, we become **autotelic**, relying less on external rewards for our happiness because what we do normally becomes naturally rewarding.

Finding the Balance between Skills and Challenges

Lastly, peak experiences occur most often when people are participating in an activity that's not so difficult as to cause frustration, yet not so easy as to induce boredom. Flow occurs in the sweet spot where our skills are just the perfect match for the challenge, and where the challenge is greater than our everyday experiences. So when facing a challenging task, you may want to increase your level of skill or gather the resources to help you tackle it. If the task is too mundane, you may want to increase the difficulty of the activity or add complexity.

An Example from the Assembly Line

We can see all three of these approaches at work in one of my favorite examples from Csikszentmihalyi's book *Flow*. He describes an assembly line worker who has to perform the same mundane task every day. The task is supposed to take no more than 43 seconds to complete. This equates to performing the task over 600 times in a working day. But over the last five years, instead of growing tired of this job, the worker enjoys it because he has turned it into a game. He performs the task with the intent of trying to beat his best time.

The worker describes his experience performing this task the same way a dancer describes being in flow while dancing, the same way a golfer describes being in the zone while on a golf course. He is able to engage in his job with a clear goal (beat my best time), and has found a way to make it intrinsically enjoyable and appropriately challenging.

Instead of focusing on the fact that he had to spend his entire day doing what some would consider a mundane task, the assembly line worker focused simply on one task at a time, with the goal of each task being to beat his old speed record.

We can do the same with any activity we have to perform. In other words, we can turn anything we do into a game.

We can reframe any activity to spark our interest or competitive nature. We can turn a simple task into a challenge by creating rules that have to be followed. We can simplify a daunting task by chopping it up into smaller tasks that we can approach more easily – or first develop the skills to handle it better, or gather resources such as tools and help from others. Working on softball drills might become tedious, but it might make playing in a game more fun.

All these strategies are simply ways to focus our attention so that we have a more integrated self, which is the epitome of the flow state. As Csikszentmihalyi wrote in *Flow*:

"Flow helps to integrate the self because in the state of deep concentration consciousness is unusually well ordered. Thoughts, intentions, feelings, and all the senses are focused on the same goal. Experience is in harmony."

Hence, flow is when consciousness works smoothly rather than being interrupted by our own questions and doubts.

Solitude and Leisure Activities

I use to think I desired solitude because I wanted an escape from stress. But from the perspective of flow, maybe what I really desire is a smoother consciousness. If this is the case, then I may not just be looking for a reprieve from stress triggers, but from having my attention pulled in several different directions. The irony is that many of us are conditioned to value multitasking, being constantly informed, and being continuously connected to our electronic devices.

Think of how some people absolutely need to have the radio on while driving. Think of how we have become a culture addicted to being constantly on the cutting edge of news reports, Facebook updates, Twitter feeds, and emails. Some people cannot be in their own house alone without the television on, even if it is only there as background noise. It's as if some of us can't live by ourselves. Or maybe some of us just can't live *with* ourselves.

The irony, then, is that our desire for solitude may be the desire to escape the distractions that often bombard our consciousness, pulling it apart in so many different directions. We want to experience a more focused state of consciousness.

This could be why so many people turn to activities like watching television, watching films, or playing video games. These help focus our attention and stimulate us in ways that give us pleasure.

However, in many flow studies, people who participate in these sorts of leisure activities do not often use words like "gratifying" or "satisfying" to describe their experience. Though they may report losing themselves in the activity and losing track of time, they often don't describe their experience as being meaningful.

These leisure activities do not often induce flow. But because we are desperate for ordered attention, we may turn to them anyway as a quick solution.

In addition to these leisure activities, you may want to simply unplug and rest. Leave the computer alone, your television off, and detach yourself from your mobile device. Resist the urge to be busy. What you may find is that rather than struggle to find flow experiences, you're more likely to attract them. Your mind can now be free to spontaneously think of endeavors that will be more gratifying or meaningful.

This may be a reason why we turn to these leisure activities in the first place: to avoid doing what is really of value to us because we fear failure and disappointment. This is a topic we'll discuss more in my last email.

Living Smooth

Use the idea of *smooth* as a reminder to engage the world in a way that captivates you. Use it as a reminder that there are ways to approach life – especially activities we feel forced to participate in – that allow us to feel deep satisfaction from our efforts.

The approaches I've shared here primarily come from psychological research on flow and peak experiences. But even without being familiar with this research, don't you have the feeling that you are already intuitively familiar with this approach to life? Isn't there another term to describe participating in life so that we avoid bore-dom and frustration, one where we have a clear goal in mind, where we participate simply for the love of it?

Isn't it called "play"?

Play: *engage in activity for enjoyment and recreation rather than a serious or practical purpose.*

We are naturals at this when we are young. We are born with a great desire to play. And I find it interesting that it is at this point in our lives when a majority of us are the most creative, the most enthralled with life, and the most consistently happy.

Many psychologists see the innate drive for children to play and theorize that these experiences help us build skills to better han-dle life. Play helps build social skills, problem-solving skills, skills needed to be resilient, amongst many others. However, we might be missing a really important alternative view of play.

In addition to childhood play building skills that enable us to thrive as an adult, it may be that play IS the optimal skill needed to thrive as an adult.

Research tells us that though life inherently has ups and downs, our consciousness can feel smooth if we simply approach our activ-ities as a game. Just as in childhood games, sometimes things in life go our way and sometimes they don't. Sometimes we have a bad roll of the die, land on a bad location in a board game, or make a bad move. To best enjoy and do best in a game, one can't live and die with every setback. Studies show that stress and anxiety will make your performance suffer. Maybe we should take the same approach in life in general.

Think about athletes who are in the zone. It's not that they do everything perfectly. It's that their consciousness is so focused on success, that when they do experience a failure they see it as an ab-erration and quickly move on.

The key then isn't to *not* pursue practical endeavors. It is a mat-ter of *how* you pursue them.

Many children lose more than they win, but due to the inherent gratification that comes with playing a game they will play again anyway. As they say, it isn't whether you win or lose, but how you play the game that makes the experience a satisfying one and compels you to give it another go. Wouldn't it be nice if our experience of life were more this way?

Since it's okay for an adult to *play an instrument* and *play a sport*, maybe we should make a greater attempt as adults to *play* life.

If we engage in our activities with the joy of a child in a game, if we discover more creative solutions to problems and become more satisfied with our lives, then who cares what others think about our unconventional playfulness? Our results will speak for themselves.

-JW

Live Meaningfully
Email
7

Meaningful (adjective):
Having real importance or value.

" A meaningful life."

 Sent on 10/21/2013 7:37 PM

Hi, Vickay,

I haven't heard from you in quite a while. I can only hope you are doing well and that what I've shared in the past several emails has been useful to you in some way. In this email, we will be focused on the skill of living meaningfully. As you might guess, I have lots to share with you from my notes concerning this topic. I encourage you to read this in small chunks, though I'm sending it whole.

A part of me is a bit sad as I am typing these words, since it's really the last email I'm planning to write. You might be surprised to hear this, but I owe you a debt of gratitude.

As I mentioned to you when we started our email exchanges, I am in the middle of putting together a textbook for my *Psychology of Happiness* course. However, what I didn't mention was that I had been struggling with how I was going to approach writing it. And though much of what I've shared with you thus far has simply been from my notes, going through the process of articulating these ideas to a real person (you) has helped clarify what I would like to get across in my textbook and how I might best make it useful to my students.

So, thank you.

At first, I answered you because I found positive psychology research so useful and was eager to share this information with others. But now, as I am about to finish my intended dialogue with you, I realize that this entire experience has been much more meaningful to me than that. Just as I wrote in my last email, sometimes life provides you with experiences where you feel satisfaction with your efforts. And the past few emails I have written fall under that category.

After you've practiced living easy, light, and smooth, life may naturally feel meaningful. But I think it's worth discussing why.

Though we'll turn to psychology for further explanation, I find *living meaningfully* best expressed by mythologist Joseph Campbell:

"People say that we're searching for the meaning of life. I don't think that's it at all. I think that what we're seeking is an experience of being alive..."

What does that mean to you? What does it mean to you to have an experience of being alive? Your answer may be much more useful than any I can share.

I interact with people I think of as the walking dead every day. I'm sure you do, too. These are the people who simply go through the motions, doing whatever they think is normal or appropriate, but without individual purpose and with deadened spirits. These are people who, by definition, don't know what they're missing. From what you've written to me, I'm sure you've experienced this first-hand.

It's easy to say that the experience of peace, the feeling of joy, or the experience of flow may lead you to feel alive. But to really get it, on a gut level, it helps to look at it from the other direction – to understand what it means to feel alive by contemplating what it means to be among the walking dead.

Let's take a look at what the walking dead lack.

A Life That Matters

One of the first things I notice is that the walking dead do not see how their actions in the world are meaningful. They do not see how what they do matters. Have you ever felt that way?

I see this primarily as the result of two issues. First, because we are conditioned to live safely, we sometimes live scared. This prevents us from accepting the risks required for life's more meaningful experiences. The second is more individual and complicated: for various reasons, we can fail to experience our actions as having much influence on our own lives or on the world at large.

Leaps of Faith

You may have gotten the impression from my email on living *easy* that we should repress or turn away from unpleasant feelings. But that is far from my intention. To live easy is not a denial of negative emotions – it is a way to live our emotional life where we do not cause unnecessary suffering by misrepresenting reality or by exaggerating negative circumstances.

When we look at the meaning of our emotions, so-called *negative* emotions are part of living a meaningful life. These often indicate that we have experienced something valuable. For example, some people refuse to take on a pet because they know that eventually the pet will pass away, and they don't want to feel that pain. They prefer to abstain from feeling love because of the pain that comes with loss. But with this logic, why ever develop friendships? Why ever have children? Every love involves loss, even if not the ultimate loss. We may never develop a meaningful relationship with anyone if we always try to avoid feeling the pain of loss.

Why ever put your heart into a project, a personal goal, or a sports team if you know there's a possibility of failure that will leave you brokenhearted?

Why ever love anyone or anything?

Most people don't say categorically that they won't love, but they limit their exposure. How they do this, to what extent they do this differs. But a fearful approach to life inherently reduces our access to meaningful experiences. How can denying your chance at love and bliss be considered living? At some point, if we continually play not to lose, we're not playing at all.

What this implies is that to have a meaningful life we need courage to risk experiencing loss, disappointment, and failure. If we only participate in safe activities, life can feel trivial and meaningless.

Ride a bike with training wheels and you may feel that your actions matter little. But if you try riding a unicycle, you'll immediately know that your actions matter a lot.

Feeling that Your Actions Count

Psychology says that humans, and many other mammals, have a basic drive to "make things happen": to feel that we can influence events and outcomes. We need to see that our actions bring about some result, lead to some sort of progress. This is referred to as an **internal locus of control**.

While some of us focus on the broad question of how our actions matter in the grand scheme of things, others may simply want to feel that what they do matters in any way to anyone.

Imagine moving into the restricted grounds of a nursing home after spending most of your life free to do as you pleased. Leaving an independent life for a more dependent one can leave many feeling depressed. Living on a fixed schedule, bound to a home that is not your own, a resident can lose her internal locus of control.

A study was done to see what might influence the quality of life for nursing home residents. In the study, two groups of residents were observed. One group was given a plant to take care of in any way they saw fit. The other group was the control (baseline) group, and followed their daily schedule unaltered by the study. What the researchers noticed was that, on average, those with the plants not only reported higher levels of happiness, but they also lived longer!

The residents with the plants were able to feel as if their actions mattered again.

Think about how wonderful it feels, after changing one's diet or exercise routine, to see the results on a scale or in one's blood pressure or cholesterol readings. We can see that we are not slaves to happenstance and that we can influence the conditions of our lives.

Psychological studies show that performing altruistic acts for others has a tremendous positive effect on our own happiness. (This may sound intuitive, but from my everyday observations of people's behavior, many seem convinced that shopping at a mall is a surer path to happiness than random acts of kindness.) One reason may be that when we are altruistic we can see that our actions have an impact on the lives of others. Again, we feel that our lives matter.

This may also be why people participate in acts of destruction. Those who commit massive acts of terror, from terrorist attacks to shooting rampages in schools, may be looking for a way to feel significant. If you look at the students who perpetrate school shootings, they are often youth who felt ignored in some way, who felt that they had little control over their lives. Their acts of terror may be the result of desperately wanting to feel as if their actions matter.

What often deters us from experiencing an internal locus of control are our expectations. Imagine a man named Jim who has a goal to lose 10 pounds. Jim begins to march towards his goal by immediately making drastic changes to his diet and by exercising more intensely than ever before, finishing every session drenched in sweat. After one full week of his new lifestyle, Jim checks the scale and becomes distraught that all his work only resulted in a loss of one pound. But Jim does not give up so easily, and eats healthier and exercises harder in week two than he did in week one. At the end of the second week he checks the scale again and is shocked that his diligence was again only rewarded with a loss of one pound. Jim becomes so frustrated that he quits his new lifestyle and returns to a sedentary life full of the easy lure of fast food.

Jim set his sights on a goal that was so high that he failed to see, and failed to savor, the progress that he made. He was so focused on the goal of losing 10 pounds that he neglected to notice that his actions actually made a difference.

He failed to realize that his actions were leading him to lose a pound per week!

We often neglect to savor our baby steps, the small accomplishments that lead us to our destination. The result is that we under-appreciate the affect our behavior has on our lives, and we neglect our experience of an internal locus of control.

We also deny ourselves an internal locus of control because we take for granted the simple experiences of control that fill our daily existence. Recall the horrible conditions Jewish psychologist Viktor Frankl found himself in while imprisoned by the Nazis. Every moment of his life was dictated to him, and he lived under the constant threat of death. Yet, he writes of how he survived by letting go of what he could not control and focused his attention on what he could, including the most basic activities like how he brushed his teeth and how he chose to interact with others around him.

The activity or goal need not be grand. To have an internal locus of control, you may just need to notice the competencies you are currently displaying in your life. You may just need to become more aware of the small progress you are already making towards your goals. You may also intentionally give yourself some achievable goals to pursue that will enable you to feel this internal locus of control – completing the reorganization of your desk that you've been thinking about for weeks, running one mile or your first 5k race, completing a simple to-do list, etc.

This may sound like a simple process, but for many it may be a struggle because they will not know what goals to pursue. Identifying goals can feel like an impossible task for those who are depressed, confused, or conditioned to a life badly matched to their temperaments and talents. If you're not one of these people, this may seem like a silly problem but, believe me, it can cause the most dreadful of feelings. Worse than being a zombie going through the motions of life without a sense that your actions matter, may be being a zombie who does not move at all, lacking any direction or sense of purpose.

Sometimes the walking dead are lifeless because they have no idea what to do with their life.

The Purpose within Life

Living meaningfully requires courage to make bold choices, but it is not just setting sail and noticing how your actions have caused your ship to move. Living meaningfully requires a sense that your journey has purpose and that you are moving in a particular direction. This entails having specific, significant intentions and participating in activities that make you feel alive. I'm not referring to any grand purpose of life, but about having purpose *within* life.

Some of us are in circumstances where goals and intentions are obvious. You may have a child to take care of, a selfless cause that you are passionate about, or have other responsibilities thrust upon you. For others, this is the biggest obstacle to happiness: not knowing what purpose to give ourselves.

Campbell coined the term "following your bliss," but many are unable to. After years of suppressing their bliss some simply don't remember or can't figure out what it is.

Purpose is often provided by the social environment: our parents, our religion, popular culture. Just take inventory of popular films, television shows, and advertisements and you'll quickly get a sense of what popular culture says we should do with our lives. You can easily see our culture's definition of success.

Once upon a time, we grew up in cultures rich with ritual and ceremony that would initiate their younger members into adulthood. The initiation process would include training for assigned roles in the tribe: gather, hunt, fight, and cook. In any case the purposes within life were clearly defined for us.

Our culture, much larger and more diverse, defines purpose more loosely, and is both more appreciative of and less attentive to those who take unique paths. Now, trailblazers have a better chance of earning admiration, while at the same time many people get lost in the shuffle. One result is people struggling to find the purpose within their life. Sometimes, we are disenchanted with the purposes offered by our social environment. On one hand this is healthy, since we are exercising our freedom to think for ourselves and follow our own personal passions. For instance, not too long ago men were cast in the role of breadwinner while women were cast primarily as the homemaker. Only certain professions were meant for each gender, while blacks and other minorities were restricted to low-level jobs. Movements to break these conventions resulted in many people having more options. On the other hand, this has led some to an existential crisis.

Think about the structure of a child's life in modern, Western societies. Often from the age of 4 until the age of 18, children are given direction. They are told where they must go, when they must be there, and what to do once there. Through schooling, every day of a child's life is given purpose. But once we leave high school, our purpose may not be so clearly defined. At that point, many of us are faced with the monumental task of taking responsibility for our own purpose. We are faced with questions that our tribal ancestors had answered for them by culture. *Where do I go now? What do I do now? What kind of life should I live?*

Many of us will simply follow culture's guide, often unaware that we ever had a choice. Some are just fine with this, while others may feel empty by taking the conventional path. Our talents and interests may lead us in other directions. We might also reject conventional paths simply because we want to avoid feeling coerced by culture. Psychological studies show that we much prefer to follow intrinsic motivations than extrinsic ones. You may love to read on your own, but once it's assigned to you and are "forced" to do it, your enjoyment may not be the same.

Either way, after coming to the realization that we can choose our lives, we can feel lost in choice. No more cultural compass. No more map. We now have to decide our purpose for ourselves and must take responsibility for that decision.

Self-Actualization

For a clue on how to best make this choice, we can start by looking at research performed by psychologist Abraham Maslow. Though the term "positive psychology" was coined relatively recently, Maslow was performing related research in the 1950s. He was one of the first to suggest that psychology study human potential and wellness, and not just how to best deal with misery.

Like Freud, Maslow believed human behavior is driven by needs. But Freud seemed to believe that we are driven by needs of deficiency. If we are lacking in love, lacking attention, lacking biological needs like food, we then are motivated to do something about it. Unlike Freud, Maslow believed we are driven by both needs of deficiency and what he called **self-actualization** needs. He articulates these explicitly as needs for wholeness, richness of life, goodness, autonomy, and other types of "meta-needs."

Maslow came to this conclusion after studying the nature of successful individuals. He wanted to see what characteristic was most common among those of us who seem to excel at life. He found that those who flourish have their deficiency needs *sufficiently* met, so that they can spend more time fulfilling self-actualizing needs. In other words, happiness often follows those who pursue activities that they find virtuous, leading to some manner of growth.

Recent psychological research into multiple intelligences and character strengths provides further clues to what these activities might look like.

Utilizing Your Inherent Genius

Intelligence is commonly associated with only three types of intellectual prowess. IQ tests primarily evaluate math skills; the verbal acuity needed by lawyers, public relations and advertising experts, English teachers, journalists and other writers; and the spatial (visual) intelligence employed by architects and designers. Schools often emphasize these three intelligences. They are valued because they are associated with practical skills, many of which are important to employers. But by growing up in an environment where only three intelligences – out of an infinity of human talent – are measured, many people develop a poor self-image.

Harvard psychologist Howard Gardner proposes that we in fact have more than three types of intelligences. He has identified bodily-kinesthetic intelligence (needed to coordinate bodily movements), interpersonal intelligence (needed to understand and work effectively with others), intrapersonal intelligence (needed to deal effectively with oneself), and musical intelligence. Gardner also identifies an environmental intelligence that enables some to more intuitively understand the workings of nature.

While a person may feel unintelligent based on conventional standards, he may in fact be an underappreciated genius by another scale of measurement. In our discussion of living smooth, I mentioned that flow occurs when our skills are in balance with the difficulty of an activity. How much happier would a person be if she participated in more endeavors that allowed her to make use of her stronger intelligence?

Exercising Your Character Strengths

In addition to intellectual strengths, positive psychologists say that happiness may also be related to our use of preferred **character strengths**. After researching 2,500 years of human cultural traditions, psychologists Martin Seligman and Christopher Peterson found 24 character traits that were repeatedly extolled as praiseworthy or valuable. Seligman and Peterson categorized these character strengths into like groups that they refer to as *The Six Virtues*: courage, humanity, transcendence, temperance, justice, and wisdom and knowledge. Research into character strengths indicates that an individual is usually more inclined to some than to others.

Without going into all 24 character strengths, here are the two discoveries I find most significant:

1.   We are often happy when we are able to utilize our character strengths.
2.   We are happy when we are able to utilize our character strengths in new ways.

Three Questions for Uncovering Your Authentic Self

From Maslow's self-actualization needs, to Howard Gardner's identification of multiple intelligences, to Martin Seligman's research with character strengths, contemporary research implies that we are happy when we are authentic and fulfilling our potential.

As Maslow succinctly stated, "If you deliberately plan on being less than you are capable of being, then I warn you that you'll be unhappy for the rest of your life."

If happiness comes to those who are true to our inherent nature, maybe we should spend more time trying to better understand what our inherent nature is. The sad fact is that many of us have been conditioned by culture to ignore who we are capable of being in favor of being who others want us to be. We either never develop this awareness of ourselves, or we forget it over time.

Psychologists have devised evaluations that can help us redis-cover ourselves. I can email you links if you'd like them. But to get started, ask yourself the following three questions.

? Question #1: *What was I passionate about while growing up?*

What sorts of activities brought you great pleasure, where you were totally in flow? What activities did you always look forward to participating in, which gave you great joy?

~

Did you enjoy writing, running, acting, singing, helping out at a soup kitchen, organizing the school newspaper, or organizing the school food drive? When we were younger we didn't always find pleasure in these activities because of external rewards (recognition, social status, fulfilling cultural expectations). Instead, we found pleasure in these activities because we were inherently passionate about them.

These activities may have brought you into flow and brought you joy because they resonated with your natural genius or one of your character strengths.

? Question #2: *If I didn't have to worry about bills and responsibil-ities, if I didn't have to worry about making money, what would I love to spend my time doing today?*

Allow yourself to be bold and dream big. What types of things would you do simply for the joy of it?

~

Envision yourself actually doing it, whatever "it" is. For many of us, just the mere thought of spending our time on these activities can produce a jolt within our system and make a giddy smile cross our faces. What if you really were to drive a race car, perform at a dance recital, go a few rounds in a boxing ring, or write a poem that gets published?

Why not pursue it? The more fearful our response to an idea, the more meaningful it may be to us. But of course, the more important a passion is to us, the more courage it requires.

? **Question #3**: *What if I knew that today was going to be my last? If I knew death would greet me tomorrow, how would I want to live my life today?*

The truth is we don't know when we will die, but we know we eventually will. Death is inevitable, but many of us ignore its impending arrival, living as if we have an endless amount of time in this world. But, if today truly were your last, what would you do? How would you use your last moments on Earth?

~

The point of all these questions isn't to inspire you to pursue a new career, though that could happen. They aren't meant to compel you to completely reorganize your life to pursue your passions, though some people do. These questions are also not meant to motivate you to curl up into a ball or spend every single second with your loved ones. They are meant to encourage you to realize how important your loved ones are to you. They are meant to help you refocus and think about what is most important in your life, since much of our attention is spent on the periphery of life.

These questions are meant to guide you towards recognizing what kind of life you really want to live, what activities are worth incorporating into your life in order for you to feel more alive.

I also hope these questions make clear what goals are worth your courageous pursuit. But don't fall into the common trap associated with pursuing goals: the belief that the whole point is to attain the goal. This attitude can easily lead to suffering. We can suffer due to craving something we don't have, experiencing the pursuit as frustration or deprivation. Then, once the goal is attained, we can become obsessed with the fear of losing it. We can feel disappointed and hungry because success didn't bring us the joy we expected. Or, the good feelings can wear off, and we might start to crave *more* – more money, a newer, more exciting spouse, greater status: once again caught in the hedonic treadmill.

Can you think of something that you craved and thought you had to have? Can you remember a time when your pursuit of this goal caused you to suffer in any of these ways?

All this can be avoided by having a different perspective on the purpose of goals.

You can think of goals as flow inducers. By being clear on what it is you want to experience in life, you are opening yourself to flow experiences. Csikszentmihalyi explains that having meaningful goals and a clear sense of purpose is essential to attaining flow. But think, for a second, why that is. Goals act as a magnet, attracting all your attention. Away go your negative thoughts because there's no room in for them in your awareness. Instead of worrying about how close or how far away you are from your goal, your focus is on the present moment. It may seem counterintuitive at first glance, but to live meaningfully, goals should not draw your attention towards the future. Setting intentions and goals are really a way for you to become completely engaged in what you are doing right now.

Second, setting goals can help us experience an internal locus of control. It's not so important whether you master the piano piece that you've set your sights on. It's important to experience the progress of mastery that you will feel along the way.

Third, what I have been writing about in this email hasn't been so much about attaining goals as it has been about clarifying the priorities of your life. Thinking about goals allows us to reflect on the type of life we want to live. Getting to know yourself in this way will hopefully allow you to fill your life with more meaningful activities, or allow you to better appreciate how meaningful your current endeavors are. I bet your life is full of meaningful activities. It's just that sometimes we get so used to them that we forget the real reason why we are participating in them – from work to school to our relationships. All you may need to experience purpose within your life is to remember what your original motivations were in the first place.

Goals and intentions should not be thought about as ends in themselves, but as sources of energy that also provide direction so we can feel we are participating in a life worth living.

Experiencing a Life Full of Meaning

As you've probably noticed by now, a lot of what we've discussed over the last four emails is about changing the context within which we experience our lives. It's not so much about changing the world around us. It is about choosing a different lens with which to perceive the world we currently live in.

The walking dead do not seem able to do this. The walking dead plod with their eyes closed, convinced that they already know what they will see if they open them. They often seem stuck experiencing the world a certain way, trudging along as if in a trance. You can try encouraging them to open their eyes to new experiences or to adopt a more optimistic outlook, but their insistence that they *already know* the world will not allow them to see the world in any other way. Much of this is due to sensory adaptation, as I mentioned earlier. We can become so accustomed to our dominant perception of the world that over time we begin to take it for granted (to forget) how interesting, unique, and abundant with possibilities the world really is. Just like becoming so used to the flavor of a new dish over time that it loses its initial appeal, the flavors of life fade into the background as we get older.

Why do you think so many of us are so excited about the possibility of a new experience? Look at all the money and effort spent pursuing the new experiences promised by a vacation, new car, new mobile device, new self-help book, or a new romantic partner. These are all symptoms of becoming habituated to a world that our younger selves found enchanting, mysterious, full of surprise. Over the course of a life, many people become so trapped in one particular perspective that the world becomes dull, monochrome, and lifeless.

The skill of accessing multiple perspectives is also the key to experiencing a life *full of meaning.*

Accessing Multiple Meanings

Imagine a man who lives in the forest. After chopping wood for a fire, he organizes his logs by tying them together into bundles. He then notices four nearby tree stumps that all happen to be the same height, so he decides to lay one of his bundles of logs across the stumps. Years later, long after the man is gone, a new family moves into the home. While looking to enjoy the nice weather on their first day, they see logs of wood lying on tree stumps, and figure the previous owner had built a table to enjoy outdoor picnicking. Years later the house is sold to a musician who celebrates his first night in his new home with a party. As he prepares for the celebration he sees that the previous owners must have been musicians too, because to his amazement, he sees a stage built out of wood that was just large enough for him and his guitar.

So what is the bundle of logs? What does it *mean?*

From the perspective of each of the characters in the above story, it may be a stage, or a picnic table, or firewood. But in reality it is a stage AND a picnic table AND firewood, AND so much more. The bundle of logs becomes more full of meaning as we think of it from different perspectives.

And isn't this true of everything, including life itself?

To live meaningfully, maybe we don't necessarily need to find the meaning of life in an absolute sense. Maybe we simply need to learn to experience life *as already* full of meaning.

When we were children, we experienced an inherently meaningful world simply because we knew we did not *know* life. We were literally seeing the world with fresh eyes and found ourselves continually in awe of it. The decades pass, and through habituation, people come to feel as if they know the world –but that is far from the truth. The world is so vast and diverse, so ever-changing, that there's no reason it shouldn't be as mysterious to an adult as it is to a child. Our adult perception may be even more capable of appreciating the mystery if we can be courageous enough to face the constant uncertainty of life. It is only through acknowledging how little we know about the world that we ever put ourselves in the position to learning anything new. According to physicist Albert Einstein, this sense of unknowing is not just critical to the pursuit of knowledge but to life itself.

> The most beautiful thing we can experience is the mysterious. It is the source of all true art and science. He to whom this emotion is a stranger, who can no longer pause to wonder and stand rapt in awe, is as good as dead: his eyes are closed.

We can choose to open our eyes by realizing there is more to the world than the way we currently experience it. We can try to see the world through different perspectives. For example, in my creativity class, I ask my students to explain how a pen might be used differently by a writer, science teacher, gardener, and chef. The world can look different depending on the goals you are trying to achieve in life.

You can take the same approach with your experience of life in general. How different would your life feel if you looked at it from the perspective of someone with circumstances drastically worse than your own? How different would your daily routine be if you imagined yourself experiencing it for the first time? What might it feel like to go through your day as if you were experiencing the world for the last time? The world can feel different depending on the context with which you perceive it.

What might a physicist's, biologist's, or chemist's account of life sound like? How would those differ from a more mythic or spiritual account? How might life be described by a big businessman or a politician? How might this differ from the perspective of a poet? The world can look different depending on the language you are using to describe it.

When you take a look out through your windshield on a sunny day, what do you see? How would you describe your experience? Do you see *a sunny day*? Or do you not even experience that, with your mind so busy with thoughts about the past or the future?

Poet Haruki Murakami has experienced it this way:

The sun sliced through the windshield, sealing me in light. I closed my eyes and felt the warmth on my eyelids.

Sunlight traveled a long distance to reach this planet; an infinitesimal portion of that sunlight was enough to warm my eyelids.

I was moved.

That something as insignificant as an eyelid had its place in the workings on the universe, that the cosmic order did not overlook this momentary fact.

Every moment of our lives can be enlivened by seeing the world from a different perspective. And as we've already discussed, some perspectives are more useful and empowering than others.

When we linger on an unpleasant event or circumstance, a change of context can diffuse them. For example, some people think of life as a test with challenges that lead to growth or as a classroom with obstacles meant for learning new lessons. Others believe in a higher power, the natural intelligence of life, or in a purposeful universe. All of these contexts give our difficult experiences meaning that can propel us forward, giving us the perspective that difficulties are not just random inconveniences but events that have their place in a life worth living.

Even seeing ourselves from a purely biological view can help us better deal with unpleasant circumstances. Imagine being severely criticized by another. Immediately, you feel hurt and defensive, no matter what the content of the criticism might be. Your automatic self-protection kicks in and triggers anger or shame – an automatic reaction from the more impulsive parts of our brain. If you can focus your attention on this objective, biological perspective (*this anger is a chemical reaction that I can let fade*), you can avoid personalizing the matter and becoming trapped in an unproductive internal dialogue (*that bastard, how could he say that*). Instead, you can look at the criticism as a new piece of information and consciously decide what to do with it. It may be worth taking to heart or it may not be, but you won't know unless you listen to the criticism itself, rather than your response to the criticism. This biological perspective can help us be more objective about the circumstances that cause us pain.

Through practice, seeing the world through multiple contexts not only helps us in the moment, but builds resiliency for the future. When moving into a cabin in the woods, why only see a table if what you need is a small stage? Or more to the point, why ever limit vision to only one of these perspectives, when you can see both for free?

Compassion: Making the World Come Alive

I find it interesting what types of perspectives our species has most often gravitated towards to fill our lives with meaning. A quick survey of the world's religions and mythologies shows that we have often seen ourselves as part of a greater whole. More specifically, we have often seen ourselves as being part of a world that itself participates in meaningful activity.

In addition to wanting the personal experience of being alive, we seem to want to feel that the *whole world around us*, that we are a part of, is itself also alive.

Some psychologists say this stems from our need to make sense of the world. Experiments in cognition illustrate that human beings are born meaning makers. We have an impulse to find patterns and make sense out of a chaotic world. We naturally take random pieces of information and impose a story on the information, tying it together so that we can feel safe in a world we think we understand. To believe the world itself participates in purposeful activity is a way for us to make sense out of the chaos around us. However, I think it may also be related to other psychological factors.

Up to this point, I have neglected to emphasize what studies indicate has the greatest effect on our level of happiness. More than money, education, or even health, it is the strength of our social networks that has the most profound correlation with happiness. We feel best when we feel connected to others.

One explanation for this comes from the long past of our species. We evolved to live within communities. There are lots of fascinating studies exploring exactly what triggered the explosive growth of the human brain – what makes us different from all those we share the planet with – but though the *what came first part* is still under debate, the fact that intelligence and language are very, very useful in social life is clearly important. In order to survive, we needed to coexist with our parents and extended family group; in order to succeed in the larger community of highly intelligent primates, we needed to understand how others think, what they want, what they fear. Understanding others as like us and different from us, learning to communicate and remember what others have told us, was such a brilliant success, that it's no wonder that we would want to extend this even further, wanting to experience connection to the world of nature, weather, time, the celestial bodies, and the realm of the invisible and imagined.

Another explanation stems from our own early experiences. What are these? You may not remember it, but your earliest sensations and feelings happened in your mother's womb, when your body was part of the body of another human being. In fact, there was probably no sense of "I" and "other" during these early stages of our conscious development. We *were* our mothers – literally part of a greater whole that was also very much alive with purpose.

Some psychiatrists, such as Stanislav Grof, believe these perinatal experiences can profoundly influence our psychological makeup. Could it be then that the human tendency to see ourselves as part of a greater whole that is itself alive is an echo of these early experiences? Could this explain why we desire to experience the universe as alive, because in our beginnings, this was literally true?

When we look at many of the characteristics of a happy life – forgiveness, sharing joys with others, strong social networks, altruism – we see a picture of a species that comes naturally to compassion. Might this be related to our earliest experiences, living in and with our mothers in a state of unconditional love? Is our search for meaning related to our need to love and be loved as we were in our mother's womb? Is our desire for an enlivened world part of an underlying need to love the world and to sense that the world (as a whole) loves us back?

Obviously, this is the philosopher in me asking questions and I often find asking questions more useful than actually answering them. At the very least, these questions go to show that there are many ways of experiencing the meaning of our lives.

Living Meaningfully

What I've shared are the ponderings of a humanities instructor who wants you to be an active explorer of your own life. I can't know what of all that I've said will resonate with you, whether you will be impelled to make big changes or simply look differently at the future of your life. Nor do I have any idea what you will do with these emails, or if you are reading them at all. But I have still found the experience meaningful to me.

And even if you have been reading them, I have no idea what meaning you will make. This is a good thing. It means you have the freedom to create ways of seeing, thinking and living that I may not be able to imagine. By doing so, you will have found ways of making these emails meaningful to you.

Take the information I've given you and make it your own. It was never mine to give you in the first place.

I look forward to hearing from you again in the near future.

Best wishes,
-JW

Part

III

Epilogue

Dear Professor,

'm so sorry it's taken so long for me to email you back. By now, you probably regret responding to my first emails. You probably hate me for not sending you feedback as I promised. For all I know, you've lost interest in hearing what I have to say. But just in case you do read this, I want you to know how important your emails have been to me. I hope you believe me when I tell you that I was so caught up in each one that I don't know if I would have had anything to say, even if I were able to write back to you earlier.

With all of that said, I have three confessions to make.

The first, and I'm embarrassed to say this, is that for the past several weeks I have had many sleepless nights reflecting on your emails and how they relate to my own life. (That's not exactly what I had in mind when I first reached out to you.) My mind has been full of doubt and regret – doubting whether I can make changes in my life and regretting my past decisions and behaviors. In spite of these worries, I've continued to try to become more mindful of how I am living my life now, but I struggle every day. I'll find myself caught up in the negativity you talk about. Sometimes I'll catch myself getting huffy and self-righteous about people who crossed me in some way. Sometimes I'll still feel imprisoned by my unhappiness. Sometimes I get caught up worrying, thinking my only escape is through a back door parole.

But every once and a while, in the middle of these thoughts, I'll realize something interesting. I notice that I'm aware of being caught up in my thoughts. I'll even sometimes say to myself, "Hey, Vickay, there you go worrying and fearing again." And once I have that kind of thought, I can ask myself, "Do I prefer this experience or would I rather be happy?"

When I have the juice, I choose happiness. But honestly, sometimes it feels good to choose anger, or stress, or frustration, or worry.

I don't know why, but it does. It brings a rush of pleasure. Even when I know it's bad for me, it feels good, and sometimes it feels good *because* it feels bad. But the point is, sometimes I actually do experience having the choice. And though I may not choose happiness, realizing that I am aware enough to see I have a choice makes me happy.

Also, knowing that I have experienced choice makes me feel that my struggles are leading somewhere, that my attempts to practice living differently have actually made a difference. It gives me hope for the possibility of more consistent happiness.

Does any of this make sense?

Here's my second confession. The reason I wasn't able to email you back until now is that for the past several weeks my email privileges were taken away from me. I had found a sneaky way to print out the first of your seven emails even though I wasn't really allowed to do that, but I got caught and was given a ticket. When I shared the email with the counselor here, she was nice enough to log into my account and print out the rest of your emails for me before our weeklies. She was so supportive. I owe her thanks too.

As you might have already guessed, my second confession really is that I am currently incarcerated. I've been in prison for over three years. I don't really know anyone that has taken your course. I found your syllabus online when I was "accidentally" able to access the Internet one day. I'm sorry for not being honest sooner. I was afraid of telling you the truth. I was ashamed and embarrassed. I was afraid that you wouldn't reply back if you knew where I was, or who I was.

My third confession is that the research you shared wasn't what I found most enlightening about your emails. Don't get me wrong, the information has been more than eye-opening, but it wasn't the material you shared that most moved me. What really got to me was how you said that *I* played an important role in what you were doing in *your* life. I cried when I read that something I did was actually helpful to you. I hardly feel as if I can affect my own life. How is it possible that I could affect yours? It's crazy and I still feel funny, weird, shocked as I type this.

Living in prison, I sometimes feel like a nobody. My life doesn't matter – I'm of no use to anyone. How could I have had a positive impact on your life without being near you, without knowing anything, simply because I asked a question? It was so empowering to think that simply by having hope, by trusting myself, reaching out and not giving up, I was able to actually make your life more meaningful in some way. Being true to myself might become addicting. Is this type of addiction a bad thing?

Professor, I don't know if you've ever visited a prison, but it can be so depressing. And it's not because of my lack of freedom or because I miss the life I left behind. The worst thing about living here is that I am reminded every day of all the mistakes I've made. Some of my friends blame other people, but I think when they're by themselves they're just like me, beating myself up, asking how I got here: *Why didn't I appreciate the life I had? Why didn't I live my life differently? Why did I think I needed so much to be happy?* All of us in here brought our baggage with us, so now everyone I meet is a reminder of a decision gone wrong.

One day I started wondering how I was supposed to become a happier person if unhappiness is the norm around here. I'm not naïve to think I was put here to be happier, but I just don't see how this unhappiness helps me or anyone else in here become a better citizen. Wasn't my unhappiness the reason I wound up in here in the first place? This might sound nuts, but even though I've been convicted of a crime, I don't really consider myself a bad person. I just made a bad decision based on a bad approach to happiness. I didn't do anything violent. If you want to know, it was credit card fraud. I wasn't poor – I'd just gotten used to having what I wanted. You remember I said I once tried to live a less materialistic life? It was fine having less money for a while, then my marriage came apart, and I started buying things to feel better. And then I found a site where you can buy stolen credit card numbers... It was just what you talked about – emotional need and the addiction. I think that's true of a lot of us in this place. I just got fed up with being unhappy and took matters into my own hands, and maybe that was the key all along.

Life here can feel so meaningless. The only thing we have to look forward to is the gate, and so lots of us dream of the day when we get back our freedom. But, isn't that just the same type of thinking that got us in here in the first place? Thinking we can be happier later, that a better life is ahead only after we get the thing we want? I'm scared of the difficulties I'll face as an ex-convict. And for all I know, I might piss somebody off tomorrow, and won't have any other days ahead of me. So I'm trying to do better and appreciate the life I've got, the precious minutes in the yard with fresh air and sunlight, laughs and stories with friends who know how I feel, and my time reading emails from a person I've never met.

I guess in some perverse way being in prison has been a blessing in disguise. It's given me a chance to actually think about my life and how I live it. It's not like there's anything else important going on. I don't have many freedoms, but I still have freedom of thought. I can choose to live differently. Of course I wish I could have done this sooner, before ending up in here. Sometimes all I can think about is how little time I'll have left of my life once I'm released. But, no point regretting something I can't change, right? I've got a chance to change now, so I'll take it.

I probably wouldn't have ever thought about my life this way without prison. I wonder how much of my problems can be looked at as blessings in disguise. That would sure be helpful. In your last email on living meaningfully you emphasized the importance of seeing our lives from different perspectives. Is this an example of what you meant?

After each time I read your emails, I become more convinced that I have to reread them again. (I'm slow that way, I guess.) With each reading I feel like I have more hope for a happy life. But the deeper question I'm struggling with right now is whether or not I deserve to be happy at all.

Yikes! I've been so wrapped up in finally writing back to you that I'm almost out of email time today. If you're actually reading this, sorry to burden you with all my stuff. It's been building up the past few weeks and I did promise you feedback. Does any of what I've said so far count as feedback?

You're probably sick of sending me emails, so I promise not to bother you anymore. I wish I had something more profound to say considering all that you have kindly shared with me all these weeks. I guess the best I can do is just thank you for all my sleepless nights and hope that you don't hate me forever.

-Vickay D.M

 Sent on 11/24/2013 11:27 PM

Hi, Vickay,

I'm nearing the end of the quarter, and I was in the middle of grading papers when I noticed your email. I was a bit frazzled when I first saw it, to say the least. It took me a few minutes for it to really sink in what had arrived in my inbox. And when it did I was a little torn on what to do. A part of me was nervous, another part excited. I think it's been over two months (?) since your last email. I wasn't sure if you would ever write back. I admit to being a little frustrated that I hadn't heard from you in such a long time, but I never hated you. I was mostly worried about what you might be going through that prevented you from getting back to me. My negativity bias was alive and well.

With it getting close to finals, I don't know when I'll have another chance to write you. So I really wanted to take some time now to let you know that I was awed by what you've shared with me. All I've tried to do through my emails was to share ideas that I have found interesting. My only hope was that you could make some sense of it and find it meaningful in some way. I never imagined how you would use it, nor could I have imagined how you actually did use it.

You probably don't need any advice from me, and I don't really feel qualified to give you any, especially after learning of your circumstances. I even feel kind of silly for having sent you some of the information I did. You are much more the expert on this subject than I am, and I've learned more from you in your last email than you could have ever learned from my notes.

Instead of advice, I'll give you a few last words of encouragement.

One, it sounds like you are doing more to improve yourself while in prison than many people I know are doing outside of it. So, don't worry about how much time you'll have left to enjoy life after being released. I think with the approach you're now taking with your life, you are already giving yourself an early parole.

Anyway, as the Greek philosopher Lucretius said, "A life that is happy is better than one that is merely long."

And two, I commend you for all the progress – no matter how small – you've made so far in your new approach to life. I wish you continued success. You not only deserve to be happy, but society as a whole deserves for you to be happy.

So please, never think that you don't deserve a happy life. We all deserve one.

-JW

P.S. There's something I didn't mention earlier, which is often neglected in books on happiness, though it's taught in most introductory psychology courses. I know this is going to sound trivial compared to everything I've shared over the past few months, but it's not.

You'd be surprised how much easier it is to be happy if you simply find a way to get more sleep. ☺

Acknowledgments

No book is ever written by a single author. Every author is influenced by various people in a variety of ways whether the author is aware of it or not. So, I have many people to thank for the creation of this book.

One of the reasons I first began investigating the science of happiness was to help me better engage the students in my introductory psychology courses. My thanks go to all of my former psychology students at Heald College for being the first to inspire me to delve deeper into the study of positive psychology. Thank you to Erika Bryant, Program Director at Heald College, for giving me the opportunity to become inspired. I am also deeply grateful to my former Department Chair, Marilyn Fowler, for accepting my proposal to teach a graduate course on the psychology of happiness at John F. Kennedy University, and to the current Department Chair, Karen Jaenke, for her continued support of this class. Furthermore, this book was greatly influenced by all of the wonderful classroom discussions I've had with my philosophy and humanities students at De Anza College and John F. Kennedy University. In many ways, this book was written in honor of those discussions.

I'm also grateful for all of the diverse feedback and suggestions I've received from my friends and colleagues. My special thanks to Susanna Anderson, Christine Chiou, Rodrigo Dobry, Bernie Harris, Matt Harvey, Sarah Heath, Mischa Hepner, Lorraine Lyman, Patrick Marks, Katrina Martin, Linda H. Mastrangelo, Prasun Prakash, Marcia Estarija Silva, and Susanne West. Though I may not have heeded all of your advice, all of you provided invaluable input that helped me further develop my ideas. Additionally, this book was greatly enhanced by the contributions of my editors Marcia C. Abramson and Margaret Diehl. Thank you both for your critical eyes, excellent recommendations, and for helping me mold these emails into a book worth reading.

The folks at Stanford University's Etkin Neuroscience Lab also deserve a special mention for giving me an opportunity to "play in the lab" and for exposing me to some incredible cutting-edge research on emotion regulation. I will never forget all of the humbling lab meetings, the joys of applying electrode gel into people's caps, and the fun of washing my hair in the bathroom sink.

Lastly, I'd like to thank Professor J.W. and Vickay D.M. for sharing their intimate email exchanges with me. I couldn't have written this book without you.

References

Achor, S. (2010). *The Happiness Advantage: The Seven Principles of Positive Psychology That Fuel Success and Performance at Work*. New York: Crown Business.

Begley, S. (2007). *Train Your Mind, Change Your Brain*. New York: Ballantine.

Ben-Shahar, T. (2007). *Happier: Learn the Secrets to Daily Joy and Lasting Fulfillment*. New York: McGraw-Hill.

Bryant, F.B. (2003). *Savoring: A New Model of Positive Experience*. Mahwah, New Jersey: Lawrence Erlbaum Associates.

Campbell, J. & Moyers, B. (1988). *The Power of Myth*. New York: Doubleday.

Csikszentmihalyi, M. (2008). *Flow: The Psychology of Optimal Experience*. New York: HarperCollins Publishers.

Dalai Lama. Cutler, H. (1998). *The Art of Happiness: A Handbook for Living*. New York: Riverhead.

Diener, E., & Biswas-Diener, R. (2008). *Happiness: Unlocking the Mysteries of Psychological Wealth*. Malden, MA: Blackwell Publishing.

Emmons, R. (2007). *Thanks!: How the new science of gratitude can make you happier*. Boston: Houghton Mifflin Co.

Gardner, H. (2011). *Frames of Mind: The Theory of Multiple Intelligences*. New York: Basic Books.

Frankl, V. (2006). *Man's Search for Meaning*. Boston: Beacon Press.

Fredrickson, B.L. (2009). *Positivity*. New York: Crown Publishers.

Gilbert, D. (2007). *Stumbling on Happiness*. New York: Vintage Books.

Goldeman, D. (2003). *Destructive Emotions: How Can We Overcome Them?* New York: Bantam.

Haidt, J. (2006). *The Happiness Hypothesis: Finding Modern Truth in Ancient Wisdom*. New York: Basic Books.

Hanson, R. (2009). *Buddha's Brain: The Practical Neuroscience of Happiness, Love, and Wisdom*. Oakland: New Harbinger Publications.

Holden, R. (1998). *Happiness Now!* London: Coronet Books.

Lyubomirsky, S. (2008). *The How of Happiness: A Scientific Approach to Getting the Life You Want*. New York: Penguin Press.

McDougall, C. (2009). *Born to Run: a Hidden Tribe, Superathletes, and the Greatest Race the World Has Never Seen*. New York: Alfred A. Knopf.

Myers, D. (1993). *The Pursuit of Happiness: Discovering the Pathway to Fulfillment, Well-being, and Enduring Personal Joy*. New York: Avon Books.

O'Connor, R. (2008). *Happy at Last: The Thinking Person's Guide to Finding Joy*. New York: St. Martin's Press.

Peterson, C., & Seligman, M. (2004). *Character Strengths and Virtues: A Handbook and Classification*. Oxford: Oxford University Press.

Post, S., & Neimark, J. (2007). *Why Good Things Happen to Good People*. New York, NY: Broadway Books.

Provine, R. (2003). *Laughter: A Scientific Investigation*. New York: Viking.

Richard, M. (2006). *Happiness: A Guide to Developing Life's Most Important* Skill. New York: Little, Brown, & Co.

Seligman, M. (2003). *Authentic Happiness: Using the New Positive Psychology to Realize Your Potential for Lasting Fulfillment*. New York: Free Press.

Uhl, A. (2008). *The Complete Idiot's Guide to the Psychology of Happiness*. New York: Alpha Books.

About the Author

Javy W. Galindo, M.A., M.Eng.,

is a professor of philosophy, humanities, and psychology in Northern California. This former electrical engineer and performing arts instructor is also the author of a creative thinking text, *The Power of Thinking Differently: An imaginative guide to creativity, change, and the discovery of new ideas.*

Made in the USA
San Bernardino, CA
09 December 2014